Medieval Millionaire

Anonymous Wealth

Betterment House Publishing

Medieval Millionaire

Betterment House Publishing
www.BettermentHousePublishing.com

6   5   4   3   2   1
ISBN 978-1-5023-1710-0

for UNK

Table of Contents

A LETTER TO
THE READER

ear Reader,

    Thank you for taking an interest in the *Medieval Millionaire*. It's a decision that could change your life.

The information in this book is product of in-depth retrospection and analysis of the path that I took to become the man that I wanted to be, and to have the financial independence that I so badly desired. This book is a radical approach to becoming wealthy, and is intended to help one affect a comprehensive change of self and life, with a strengthening of finances being only a part of the reward.

    I did not come from money; far from it, in fact. However, as I grew up, I did not let my past shackle me to a future I didn't want, and instead used every life lesson I could recognize to become someone that was successful and self-sufficient–financially and otherwise–all while I was still in my twenties.

I believe that every person has the right to be happy, healthy, and to lead the lifestyle they desire, provided it does not prevent another from doing the same. As I do in my life, I believe that these are qualities of life that any-one can work towards, if he or she knows that they're available to him or her and which way to go. I believe that we live in an age where most people give up too easily and reinforce to themselves they don't have the power to take control of their lives. I want to change that. I want to help hand the reins over to the people that are seeking something more. That is what this book is intended to accomplish.

I published anonymously for two reasons. First and foremost, I have no desire for added outside attention. I am a self-proclaimed introvert and I have never been one that sought fame, just fortune. With that, for the reader's sake, I don't believe this book should be attached to any-one. If there is no known author to analyze and compare one's life to, then this book truly becomes a gift for the reader for he or she to use entirely as he or she sees fit. You must determine the path that you desire and feel is right, and that is not done by emulating the lives of those that have come before you.

Medieval Millionaire, in fact, has little need for an author's personal involvement at all, regardless of anony-mity. This book is devoid of inspirational stories or blatant name-dropping. True, all the information is derived from hard learned life lessons, and there is the rare passage that I mention what I have personally done, but the information is presented in a manner that is fairly objective, concise, and structured, and the personal additions are only included as potentially helpful examples. I do not give you my life story and then say, "Here you go, just do as I did." Instead, I have painstakingly taken the time to deconstruct exactly what aspects of my self, lifestyle, and perspective that made and continue to maintain my personal and financial success, and I have organized them in such a way so that anyone can apply them to just about any lifestyle, regardless of background or personality.

I suspect that my anonymity will cause suspicion in some. The question no doubt will be raised of what qualifications I have to give people advice on wealth if I refuse to expose myself for public scrutiny. It's a valid point, and had I written a real estate investment book or a book on stocks and bonds then I would whole-heartedly agree that the person giving such precise and potentially drastic money advice should be closely examined in order to determine his or her authority on the subject. Any book that claims to be able to help someone become a millionaire should be met with skepticism and scrutiny, including this one. Unfortunately for most people, finances are the most important aspect one's life. Taking a risk on someone else's financial advice with your own money, regardless of his or her authority on the subject, can end in catastrophe. I expect and encourage the wariness of my readers; this book is not intended for those that blindly follow self-proclaimed prophets, regardless of genre. So I will tell you that the only financial risk posed by this book and the contents within is nothing more than the purchase price of this book.

I make no call to action to invest your money here, or to purchase that, or to start this type of company. This book doesn't deal with any specific markets or industries whatsoever, and the specific money advice that is provided deals only with suggested organizations of one's personal accounts, as large or little as they may be. Thus, my financial credentials are not necessary. This is a book for you, about you, and I illuminate paradigm changes in lifestyle and perspective that if followed and practiced correctly can result in wealth, if that is what you want. If you read this book and find that there is nothing to take away, then I have done a very bad job, but I have not spent years of reflection and analysis and months of tireless writing and editing to deliver a couple hundred pages of garbage.

All one has to potentially lose is the purchase price of this book. What you have to gain is up to. I have provided all the tools that I know exist that can be used to become wealthy, financially and in quality of life. You must test their validity for yourself.

This path will not be easy. I am asking you to evaluate every aspect of yourself in order to discard that which serves no positive purpose and refine the aspects of yourself that will allow you to take control of your life. I am asking you to change the way you see your relationship with money and your relationships with others. I am asking you to discard your pride. These are difficult changes to make, as you will be challenged from both within yourself as you continue your metamorphosis, and from the world around you as you begin to enact your will with your new-found power. But the world will challenge and confront you regardless of what you are doing in life, so I argue that it is better to already be fighting for what matters than to sit back and accept what happens. And remember that as tough as the world can be at times, there is at least one person, though unknown to you, that wants nothing more than for you to succeed and prosper.

So take this book, read it, try it on. Your path of attaining and keeping a wealthy lifestyle will be a lifelong journey, so if you don't absorb all that's between these pages immediately, *Medieval Millionaire* will always be there for you to return to when you're ready. I hope the best for you, in your finances and otherwise.

With well wishes for your future,

Anonymous Wealth

Medieval Millionaire

CHAPTER 1

The Medieval Millionaire, the Book

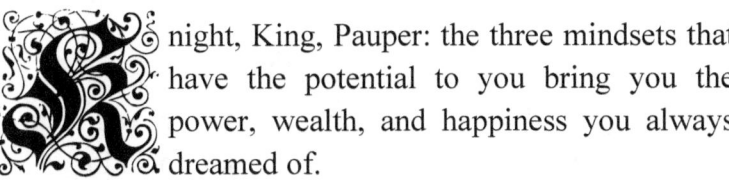 night, King, Pauper: the three mindsets that have the potential to you bring you the power, wealth, and happiness you always dreamed of.

What is *Medieval Millionaire*? It may be easier to first explain what it is not.

Medieval Millionaire is not a get rich quick scheme. It won't show you shortcuts on the Internet or loopholes in the law that will make you millions overnight. This book isn't a market guide; it's not going to tell you where to put your money. In fact, *Medieval Millionaire* isn't a book about money.

If that's the case, then what business does it have touting that it can help anyone become a millionaire? True, I only specifically address money in one chapter, but *Medieval Millionaire* has sidestepped the usual route of self-help finance books and gone straight to the source.

Where most financial books help ordinary, un-wealthy people do things with their money that might make them rich (though those that become rich are usually very lucky or in fact embody a certain amount of some of the qualities addressed in this book), they usually do nothing for the person beyond the direct, specific financial advice. These books can be very helpful in educating one in what might be best to do with his or her resources, but they cannot be treated as a magic pill that one can take to become the person he or she has imagined him- or herself to be with the life to go with it, as they so often are.

People without wealth see those with wealth and power, notice the difference in size of bank accounts, and assume that the difference between being where they are and being wealthy and powerful is just the amount of digits in annual income. Naturally, they look for information on how to make more money. But the difference between the wealthy and the non-wealthy isn't money. In fact, money is just a symptom of the difference.

If you think that you just want money, then this book may not be for you, though I implore you to at least make it through the next chapter, titled: "Of Money." Money can be found, made, and lucked upon in an amazing number of places, and there are plenty of books that will tell you where to look. But money does not necessitate wealth, and it definitely doesn't equal legitimate power or lasting happiness. If you want more than just money, that is, if you want a life where you are as confident, powerful, happy, and wealthy both financially and in quality of life as those elite that you so aspire to join, then this book will show you how you can get there.

Medieval Millionaire is about the way of thinking, the way of acting, and the way of pushing through life that, if fully embodied into one's life, can result in accruing money. This book is about becoming a quality of person with a perspective and lifestyle that has the legitimate wealth, power, and happiness that so many so badly desire. This book is about transforming ordinary people into the extraordinary. If you want to be rich–that is, if you want to only add digits to your bank account–then go buy a lottery ticket, and good luck on your chances. However, if you want to be wealthy, if you want to be a person that is respected and followed because of your strength and charisma, and has no want for material resources or emotional fulfillment, then read this book. Some of you may say that there is no difference between being rich and being wealthy. Those very real differences will be explored in the following chapter.

Aside from this chapter, the chapter on money, and the concluding section, this book is divided up into three sections, and subsequently three major shifts of perspective and lifestyle. They are personified as the archetypes of the Knight, the King, and the Pauper. This no doubt illuminates the origin of the name *Medieval Millionaire*. The order of the Knight first, King second, and finally Pauper is intentional. One must learn, understand, and begin to embody the previous before starting on the next, and all three must be embodied within the individual equally in order to fully reap the benefits of any one archetype. It is through adopting and developing the roles of each of these characters into one's own life that will lead to you developing what I refer to as the Life Success Triangle.

To put simply, the three corners of the triangle are strength, judiciousness, and empathy, represented by the Knight, the King, and the Pauper respectively. While you might recognize that you have certain strengths or predispositions towards one or the other, it is in embodying all three archetypes equally that can allow you to become a true Medieval Millionaire, with the life and self you desire.

These will not be easy transitions—no radical change of life and self is. You will have to take control of your life with 100% accountability; you will have to control your greed and responsibly invest your time, energy and material resources; and you will have to destroy any sense of entitlement. This book will guide you and illuminate how you can break up the path to wealth into small, manageable steps. I make no guarantee of anything; this transformation is up to you. It's hard work, yes, but remember that there are many that have come before you that have walked down a similar path and undergone similar transformations, myself included. If you continue to work hard and keep your eye on the path ahead of you, then you have the ability to climb to the top, as so many others have. You can have the money you've always dreamed of, but more than that, the monetary wealth will be nothing more than a mere side effect of a wealth of mind, heart, and ability, resulting in you becoming the best version of yourself that you have ever been.

If you're ready to take control of your life and your finances, then it's time for you to begin. It's time for you to become the Medieval Millionaire.

CHAPTER 2

Of Money

efore I even touch on any of the concepts further in this book, there is one idea that I need to present and that you need to integrate into your very being before you can have a hope of succeeding in your finances. Brace yourself:

Money is not what you want.

Wait, what? That's right. You do not want money. In fact, if you are not wealthy already, I would venture to say that you don't even really know what money is, or rather is not. Money is nothing more than little pieces of metal and cloth (or paper) and plastic. Money is nothing more than numbers on a computer screen or in a bank statement. The dollar bill is a promise from the United States Treasury that it is worth something, though the value isn't even concrete. Money is not happiness, money is not power, and–wait for it–money is not wealth. For you to become and stay wealthy, you must more than understand this, you have to know it in every fiber of your being. This may seem impossible and in fact irrational, but it isn't, and I will help you shift your understanding.

The Inherent Value of Money

What is money? Is it something you can eat? Is it something you can stack on top of itself to build a home with? Does money directly provide for any of your physical and emotional needs? No. Money can be *used* to translate into goods and services that can do these things (emotional needs probably excluded), but the dollar bill itself is little more than a green piece of cotton that can surprisingly survive the washing machine.

You think you want money because you want the things that you see attached to great sums of money. You think you want money because you see those with more than you (financially and otherwise) and notice money as the most obvious defining difference. But the difference between those with wealth that continue to maintain wealth and those without has very little to nothing to do with the amount of money they may have. Let's examine a fictional lottery winner to demonstrate.

Poor Jim, Rich Jim

Our fictional character, Jim, has worked all his adult
life in construction. He works hard for his money and he
tries his best to retain it while enjoying what little comforts he can afford. He has an apartment and a truck and
is currently single. Jim has also religiously purchased a
lottery ticket every day since his 18th birthday. Though
he's not destitute, he also isn't comfortable, financially
speaking. He's a few thousand dollars a year away from
being classified as poor.

Well, after getting into his early thirties, Jim finally
gets his big break. He wins the lottery, a $70,000,000
jackpot. He takes the cash option and, after taxes, has a
nice $42,300,000 in his bank account. It's not the biggest
jackpot, but it's more money than Jim has ever seen.
What does Jim do?

Well, he's rich now. For starters, he ditches the job.
No more backbreaking, sweaty, long hours for menial
pay. He gets a new truck, the top of the line, biggest
pickup he can find, and then he gets himself a nice little
red sports coupe for fun. The apartment? No more of
that! Jim has always wanted to own land, and he goes and
buys a few thousand acre ranch and has a not so modest 4
bedroom, 4 bathroom house built with two living rooms,
a theatre, a billiards room, an indoor pool, and three-car
garage with full workshop attached.

No luxury is spared. He's got the nicest toys, the

nicest clothes, and eats the best, tastiest food. Jim's rich, why shouldn't he treat himself and live the life his money can provide? Jim gets some rich friends to spend time with, and he also gets himself a gorgeous girlfriend, one with expensive tastes, but that's ok, because Jim likes taking care of her and giving her whatever her heart desires.

For ten years Jim lives big, travelling where he likes and buying what he wants. He plays here and there at being a landowner, pretending to work. He gets a small herd of Black Angus cattle and hires on a few hands to tend to them. Life is good for Jim, but then somewhere in the twelfth year of living rich, Jim realizes that he's a little low on money... actually dangerously low. But how could that be? 42.3 million dollars was enough money to live on for the rest of his life, right? Well, if he had continued to live the life he had before winning the lottery, then yes, with plenty to spare. But that's *not* how Jim lived, and before he knows it he's lost his house, the land, the toys, the friends, *and* the girlfriend with expensive taste. He has, in fact, financially extended himself so far that he finds himself in debt with a resume that could just barely get him a job back in construction, considering he hasn't worked in twelve years. Jim is now penniless and alone, realizing that he did not have any lasting happiness, power, or wealth. He's also very, very poor.

What Happened?

Jim, like most people without a wealthy mindset, saw and treated money as the answer. He thought that the money he had gave him happiness, power and wealth. But while that might've seemed to be the case, it was short lived (relatively speaking), and true happiness, power, and wealth are things that should not be exclusively tied to a sum of money.

Quite a lot of people without money say that not having enough money causes suffering and problems, but then if they somehow land themselves some serious money, they end up with just as much, if not more, suffering and problems. Granted, Jim's example is an extreme, but that sort of scenario happens *all of the time*, with the sufferers never understanding why it happened like that. The problem lies in the perspective that people without wealth have about money.

Poor/Rich and Wealthy

This crucial difference in understanding about money is what divides those that are poor and "rich" and those that are wealthy. The only difference between those that are poor and those that are rich are how many digits are in a bank account. The difference between the poor/rich and the wealthy is that being wealthy transcends the bank accounts.

The poor/rich get money and use it as a direct translation to provide themselves with all that they want. The wealthy get money and then use it to build money machines–as in businesses and investments–that provide more money over time. The wealthy invest their resources in order to return more resources than they invested.

People with wealth, those that continue to maintain and accrue wealth, see money for exactly what it is: a tool. They know that money doesn't fix a single problem. Problems are solved with ideas and action, and money provides opportunities to implement ideas into action.

Money isn't the house; money is the hammer that builds the house. Like any other tool, it's only as good as it's used, making the way the wealthy use their money very important to them. Money isn't the fruit; money is the seed that is planted that grows into a tree that bears fruit every year.

This raises the question of where happiness, power, and wealth really come from, if not from money. You perceive the wealthy to be happy, powerful, and many seem to continue to remain wealthy, and for the most part these observations are correct. What most people don't understand is that the happiness, power, and continued wealth are product of traits that come from within the wealthy person him- or herself, not from the money and lifestyle that he or she has. The money and lifestyle are byproducts of already being happy, powerful, and having a wealthy mindset.

If you're reading this book, I can assume that you're probably not content with your financial situation. You want more. You want something bigger and better. It is possible for you to attain that, but you must realize that it comes from nowhere outside of yourself. It isn't the money–money is nothing more than what you do with it. Everything that has to do with you becoming wealthy and maintaining being wealthy comes from within you.

It isn't the money that makes the wealthy,
but the wealthy that make the money.

I know how hard it can be to change your perspective about money, especially when scrounging month to month, desperately trying to make ends meet. I was there. I didn't understand the true nature of money for the longest time. But this shift in perspective is crucial if you want to succeed financially. Unfortunately, I can't tell you this is the hardest thing you'll have to do. Becoming wealthy is a shift in lifestyle and mindset, and one must become wealthy inside him- or herself before life catches up. That is to say: you must begin to become wealthy before you can attain the money attached to it.

The first and most paramount aspect of becoming wealthy is determining what you want, why, and developing the strength and goals necessary to get you there. This constant march towards what one believes in and desires for one's life is product of the archetype of the Knight.

KNIGHT

KNIGHT

e all have our concept of the quintessential Knight in shining armor. For most of us, he is a certain combination of chivalry, courage, and strength. That is the Knight in this book as well, an archetype that you will have to embody in your own life if you are to take control of your life and thus become a millionaire.

Historically, knights were the lowest level of nobility. They swore to protect and fight for certain landowning nobles or kings. They were usually given property of their own and whatever food and other amenities they needed in exchange for their service.

The knights' code of honor, chivalry, was what made them so desirable as protectors. This code of conduct differed slightly from region to region, but there were overarching themes that all knights shared. It was by following this code that they became the embodiment of strength, perseverance, and the pursuit of truth.

In this modern translation of the Knight archetype, I will establish the specifics of these essential, unshakable qualities necessary to succeed and how they are achieved. This starts by defining and embarking on a personal quest from which all motives and goals originate from.

CHAPTER 3

The Quest

irst and foremost, the Knight fights for something more than himself. Beyond swearing himself to protect another–as in the historical concept of fighting for a king– there exists a larger quest underlying the very purpose of his life. Our Knight swears no allegiance to another, but rather to himself, and fights for the purpose he establishes and refines.

I have established that wealth is not solely attaining money but embodying an existence that continuously generates money (along with other benefits) through proper perspective and action. Proper action is a combination of careful planning and precise and dedicated execution, all while working towards what one believes is most important. Those with wealth don't scatter themselves randomly in their endeavors, trying to pull money out of cracks. They have a purpose, and a strong drive to work towards it. They establish goals that are intended to bring them closer to their purpose, and it is in their effective and efficient execution of accomplishing those goals that they generate and maintain monetary wealth.

Though perhaps more than what one initially wants to approach in trying to become wealthy, the concept of purpose is completely necessary. And perhaps as convenient as it might be for me or anyone else to tell you what the purpose for your life is and have everything make sense and come together cohesively, I won't. No one can tell another what his or her purpose may be. Everyone's path is different; everyone's understanding of the world and him- or herself is different. No one's purpose is more true than anyone else's. We as individuals have nothing more to use to understand the world by than our brains and the signals provided to them by our sensory organs; to purport that one knows the truth is foolish and nearsighted. It is up to the individual to determine what his or her highest, noblest quest may be.

The concept of ultimate higher purpose may cause discomfort for some. To accept that one has a purpose means that every action is either working towards or away from that purpose. It's a formidable aspect to embrace into one's life, as it causes one to evaluate all of his or her actions to determine whether he or she is working towards said purpose. I understand how uncomfortable that can be, as I was once there, having to become accountable for my own actions. If one has not been acting towards a purpose for most of his or her life so far, then having to account for past actions can be disheartening and overwhelming, and breaking out of comfortable established habits can be even more difficult. This can cause some to run the other direction, adamantly claiming that they have no purpose, that there is no such thing as purpose, and that they have nothing to feel negatively about with the way they are living their lives.

If you make the argument that you don't have a purpose, then in consequence you eat, drink and breathe needlessly. To eat is to fulfill a desire. To have a desire is to have a projection of the future. To fulfill a desire is to work towards a favorable concept of the future. That is a purpose, if only a minor one for an individual action. Regardless of what you may try to convince yourself of, purpose exists, and it is those that recognize that they have an overarching purpose for their lives and work towards it while constantly refining what they understand it to be that are the same ones that control the rest of the world for those that refuse to explore their own purpose. But if even with that argument you continue to believe that you have no purpose, and have no desire for purpose in your life, then don't read any further and give this book to someone that does.

Purpose is what motivates everything about one's life. It's the reason we get up in the mornings, the reason we eat, and the reason we fear death. Purpose is the primary contributor to all motives that drive our actions. With this inherent drive for *something* ingrained in each and every one of us, there is a necessity to explore what it is and why it drives us. To not do so is to remain ignorant of why we choose to live.

What good is an action if it is not performed in the scope of conscious purpose? In order to become the Knight, one's perspective must lengthen to the very end of one's foreseeable life. Today your only goals may be to have all of your physical needs met–i.e. hunger, shelter, sex–and enjoy yourself with no confrontation or suffering. Multiply that by a lifetime of days. You end up with a life that was nothing more than eating three times a day, occasionally having sex, and avoiding conflict. Is that what you want your life to be about? Becoming the Knight is about knowing what you are willing to dedicate your life towards and why. If you have nothing more than a directionless, unplanned existence, your finances will also be directionless and unplanned.

This depth of perception is paramount in how successful and driven you will become. If you can begin to define your purpose for existing–to begin to recognize the path before you, as it were–from birth until your imminent death, then your life becomes a series of filling in the space in between with goals that will help you get as close to your purpose as possible.

The beauty of purpose is that it is never attained. Goals are, but there is no end to the progress one can make in one's life and in the world. Because of this, purpose should be flexible. As one progresses in life and learns from experiences, one's understanding of what is important and good will refine and shift. This holds true for long-term goals as well. You may want one thing at one moment, but in a year's time your understanding of the world might've changed enough that you no longer want whatever that was and in fact want something else. That's ok, that's good. That means that you are on a path of exploration, of learning, and rationality. To hold onto an ideal, even when it no longer rings true in your heart, is to stagnate and prevent further development of life and self. You must constantly be finding what rings true for yourself and discarding what is false. With that understanding, your continuing development and refinement of purpose is, in actuality, an inner quest for truth.

That means that what you may so dearly believe is important today, what you know in your very being to be true and good and all that you should strive towards, may not be what you believe at some point in the future, and probably hasn't been at some point in the past. Your life in embodying the Knight will be a continuing refinement of these ideals and goals so that you are constantly at an ever-more developed understanding of the world and your role in it. While perhaps difficult to establish initially, this continuous editing of understanding becomes easier to do over time. But how to do that? And more so, how does one first develop a place to start in defining what is important?

Defining and Refining

There are many ways of defining and refining one's purpose. Life and the world around us present an endless amount of potential lessons that we can use to refine our understanding of ourselves and the world. However, the shared characteristic of any experience or practice that causes development of understanding of self and purpose is pseudo-objective reflection and analysis of self. What does this mean? It means that while you may viscerally experience everything that is present on this planet available to be experienced (a highly improbable feat), it is only moments of careful contemplation and analysis of these experiences that will yield the most important part of the experience beyond the benefit of the experience itself: the lesson. If you do not reflect upon past experiences, you do not learn.

To reflect is more than to just remember. To only remember involves recalling emotion. Emotions taint one's ability to objectively and rationally analyze. One must thus perform analysis outside of the restriction of emotion. You must attempt to view yourself as objectively and unemotionally as possible while you are actively exploring your experiences and developing your understanding and purpose. To analyze outside of the filter of emotion is not easy, and the techniques you develop will truly be your own. However, I offer three approaches that one can use individually but preferably collectively and can develop upon as he or she sees fit. They are:

- Confrontation
- Inspiration
- Meditation

All three involve some aspects of reflection and thus each has its own measure of meditation. For those of you already familiar with meditation, I think you will stand with me in my statement that meditation in any form is one of the most important practices one can use to progress as an individual. For those of you that have never meditated before, don't worry. It's something anyone can learn how to do; it's only a matter of practice and commitment.

Meditation's power comes from being almost completely to completely empty of thought and emotion and will-less for a period of time. It is in these moments of mental and emotional escape that one can explore what is necessary and beneficial in oneself or one's life and what aspects of oneself or one's life are only working to inhibit growth and positivity. It takes a little getting used to, but once comfortable with the exercise of meditating, it's easy to revisit at any time.

There are different ways to enter into a meditative state, and the one you use will be what works best for you. You need to be physically relaxed and comfortable and in a quiet environment that you feel safe in. From there it's a matter of deepening your breathing and letting the spin and rush of your thoughts calm and ebb away. Deep, slow breaths are essential; they help to calm the body and provide oxygen to the brain. Sometimes mentally focusing on a single aspect, such as your breathing, works well to get one into a meditative state, though you will need to be able to focus on other aspects in turn per the guided meditations I offer for the Inspiration and Meditation techniques. One must focus on escaping the present setting and all the clingers-on that come with it. When meditating, nothing else matters; you exist, and that is all that needs to be present.

All three techniques also provide some aspect of confrontation, though that is nothing to worry about. The Inspiration and Meditation techniques utilize a non-threatening self-imposed confrontation, where one takes aspects of oneself and life and analyzes them thoroughly and completely. There is no emotional judgment, just rational exploration. However, we start with the most outwardly confrontational of the three, which is aptly named.

CHAPTER 4

The Confrontation

In one's day-to-day interactions, one is constantly coming into contact with those that most likely think differently than oneself. It could be anything from minor preferences in taste to large aspects of one's identity such as spiritual beliefs. Many differences go unnoticed or unspoken, but some are addressed. Most often this is a natural interaction, but it is in properly using these conflicts of ideas that one can define what he or she finds to be true or false about the way he or she perceives the world.

The Confrontation is the least meditative of the three. It's also the most difficult to maintain over a longer period of time because of its potentially abrasive nature, but it may be the easiest tool for those that are extroverted, tough skinned and haven't had the opportunity to develop their ability of using the other two. The Confrontation technique can also help one test and validate developments made in the Inspiration and Meditation techniques. Confrontation technique is almost exactly as it sounds.

In the Confrontation approach, you must effectively and concisely present to another what your belief, ideal, or point is, allow the other to retort or present his or her own perspective, and then analyze the validity of his or her concepts compared to your own. It may take some back and forth discussion for each person to clarify what he or she means and is trying to say. Once you have an accurate concept of his or her idea, if said idea does not seem more true for yourself compared to your own concept, then discard it; it's your decision whether you choose to continue debating the other person. If what he or she presents rationally outweighs your own concept, then you *must* adopt his or her idea and discard your own.

This is a fairly straightforward approach, picking up and dropping concepts present in your environment via those that you interact with. You are essentially encouraging your environment to be constantly testing and trying your own understanding of anything and everything, and then making the necessary shifts in understanding and perspective to assume that which is most correct.

This *cannot* be an emotional interaction. No ego whatsoever can be attached to your understanding, perspective, or ideals. These should be rational in their entirety, regardless of how you feel about them emotionally. If you cannot defend these concepts rationally to yourself or another, then they're either false or not developed fully enough to be embraced.

Emotional arguments (we can no longer call them debates when they abandon reason) are based in motives of fear or pride. Fear comes from the uncertainty of whether one's understandings are valid or not. Interestingly, pride used in this way is a form of fear. By embracing something emotionally and feeling righteous in doing so, fear remains an undertone, existing as the chance that one may be wrong for the lack of rationally exploring the concept he or she holds so dearly onto. Whatever the form of fear, if you feel it, then as the Knight you must confront it. Fear is nothing more than the unknown rearing its head in your understanding of the world. If you confront it, if you analyze that which causes you fear and learn how to deal with it either in action or understanding, then it ceases to be able to cause fear.

You must constantly recognize the impermanence of the validity of ideas in your quest for truth, as anyone's development throughout life is grounded in continuously embracing rational concepts and discarding false understandings. Thus, you must adopt the more correct idea when presented to you. If and when this happens, it is up to you to stop the debate with the other person, explain to him or her how the concept is more valid than yours–both so that you know that you fully understand this new concept that you are embracing, and making it known to the other as well–and thank him or her for the opportunity for growth (though you do not have to word it as such). This may sound excessive, but not to admit previous wrongness and openly accept the replacing idea is restricting and irrational.

Openly professing your previous incorrect concept and embracing the new, more correct concept removes any sort of perceived social power that the individual might try to hold over you in his or her success. Being completely honest and transparent, even if still incomplete in developing a more and more true concept of reality, removes another's power over you. Shame and embarrassment only stem from being caught in doing something that you shouldn't be doing (the "shoulds" of which we'll discuss further into the Knight section), whether it's thinking a certain way or performing an action. If you express yourself completely and openly to the world around you while understanding that everything about you is on a path of refinement, then you have nothing to be ashamed or embarrassed about, as you are only acting within your most correct understanding of the world (provided your actions mirror your understandings).

Many times, especially as you progress towards a more coherent and truthful understanding of yourself and the world, concepts presented to you in opposition will actually be false, and perhaps very much so. This can be a stressful experience, depending on the intensity of the opposition. You may have moments where your current, valid understanding of things is completely different or against what everyone around you believes to be true. Remember to be strong. You must remain resolute in your quest for truth. If someone with an opposing viewpoint is less correct than you (from your perspective), regardless of how belligerent or abrasive he or she may be, it is your responsibility to hold in your mind and heart what you know to be correct. If you truly believe that your current understanding of yourself and the world is rationally accurate, hold onto that and trust your convictions. It is in trusting your convictions that will give you strength against ideological attack.

Sometimes the best thing for overly confrontational interactions as such is to just walk away and remove yourself from the situation. The power of the mind is formidable, but even it can be wrangled into submission by overwhelming influence coming from all angles. There is nothing wrong with removing toxicity and negativity from one's life. Our critics can be used to illuminate what is false within us, but it is up to us to remain strong and determine the validity of their statements.

Conversely, while it is your responsibility to present your ideas, it is *not* your responsibility to change someone else's mind. The only thing in this life that any of us can have control over is ourselves, and it would be invasive to attempt to extend that control over others, as right as we may feel we are. Anyone's knowledge is built upon and developed naturally through experience and analysis, not through heavy-handed pressure or intimidation. If another won't see things your way, regardless of what you may perceive to be as a concise, rational explanation on your part, then there is nothing more you can or should do.

Understanding or admission of defeat in validity of concepts may come after the conversation has ended, and may perhaps reveal itself in a moment of solitude and reflection. This is usual, as our minds are more apt and willing to explore other possible ideas when we are not in a threatening engagement, be it mental or otherwise. In instances such as this, it is still imperative that you openly concede defeat to the individual that caused you to change your mind–if possible–as this is the most effective way to openly and forever let go of your previous belief both within yourself and in your environment. This will be further explored in the concept of a genuine apology, but for now, the idea of delayed acceptance of another's ideas brings us to the concept of the Inspiration technique.

CHAPTER 5

The Inspiration

he Inspiration technique involves outside influence removed from actual confrontation. The lines between Confrontation and Inspiration blur as one begins to embrace ideas presented by others, yet in a removed, solitary analysis. Obviously, the root characteristic of the Inspiration technique is inspiration.

Wherever you are in life, both in the strata of society and your personal understanding of self and the world around you, there may be those that you respect and admire. They can be either directly present in your life or individuals that you know of through history or media. Regardless of the degree of separation from your life, there *is* something about them that causes you to admire and respect them. Inspirational technique involves an as objective analysis as possible of that person and yourself to determine the differences and what you desire in yourself that he or she has. This is a solitary, reflective exercise, and requires an environment in which you can find peace. The amount of time you spend will be up to you, but any amount of time, even five minutes, can provide significant progress.

Such as what I presented about meditation, first and foremost, you must be able to relax. Sit or lie somewhere that's quiet. Breathe deeply and evenly. Allow your thoughts to settle. Remove yourself from your worries and pain. Lose your fears. Exist outside of time. Once you have attained a state of tranquility, bring this other person that you respect into your mind. Begin by asking these questions:

How do you feel about this person?

Why?

What is it that causes you to respect him or her?

Why?

Don't analyze the specifics. For example, were it a basketball player, you wouldn't answer that you respect and aspire to his profound ability at making 3-pointers. Instead, you would explore how you respect his command of himself in high-stress situations and dedication to refine his skill to shine above the others. Get the picture?

Continue exploring the positive aspects of this person as much as possible. Once you have an idea of the specific traits of this other person that you admire, and you understand why it is that that these traits are admirable to you, hold on to them, either mentally or–even better–in written form, and bring yourself into your meditative field of view.

Question yourself:

Do you have any of these traits already inherent in you, if only just a little?

What is the difference in your traits or lack thereof and the traits of those you respect?

How can you get there?

Stay completely away from self reinforced negativity during this personal analysis. Remember that for the most part, human beings are generally the same collection of body parts with only minor variations. To believe that someone has something that you do not is foolish. Some may have more innate ability than you to perform a specific task, but the majority of successes are not determined by the physical hardware of a body but rather how it is used. There is an importance in being realistic about your position in life or abilities, but never doubting your power to move in any direction you choose. Anyone can be anything, it just takes work.

Focusing on negativity will do nothing to provide any insight into how you can develop, and it will only work to discourage you. Focus on the positive aspects of both the person and yourself, and focus on positive developments to better implement these skills within yourself. Don't, for instance, say: "I need to stop being so lazy." What does that mean? How does that give you a path to take? Instead, if you are concerned that you aren't as productive with your time as you'd like, give yourself a positive, productive option such as: "I need to start working on _____ (a project you've been wanting to embark on)." This way you have a solution that provides an applicable development. Whether you focus on positivity or negativity, either will spawn more of the same.

The "how" question is the most important. If you see something that you like about another person and want that for yourself then you *must* determine how to get there. These paths can either be explored via trial and error or through outside research. If you think one way might work to bring you closer to the traits that another embodies, try it. If it works, make it your own. If it doesn't, revisit the potential ways you might be able to get there. If you have a chance to interact with those that you respect, ask them. Ask them how it is that they became or are so courageous, honest, determined, etc.– whatever the trait may be. The implementation of "how" in your own life will involve a mixture of continued inner reflection and analysis, and trial implementation in your actions. This continued analysis and reflection brings us to the Meditation technique.

CHAPTER 6

The Meditation

he self-guided meditation technique that I provide prompts an in-depth yet (preferably) unattached and unemotional analysis of where one is in regards to his or her life and understanding of the world. This is the most solitary of the three, as it involves no outside provocation or analysis of another; this is truly an exploration of truth within oneself. Meditation technique allows the ever-changing self to analyze the self outside of interpretations of what one "should" be or how to get to that from the influence of those around the individual. Just like with the Inspiration technique, there is no set time for how long you should do this, but the more you do, the more progress you will make.

As typical in meditation, find a quiet spot that you can find peace in. Close your eyes, relax. You can be sitting or lying down. Allow the thoughts and emotions flying through your head to slowly soften, sliding to the back of the mind. Allow your pain of the past, fear of the future, and impatience for the present dissolve. Exist outside of emotion. Once you are in a state of relaxation with an empty mind, begin to bring up individual aspects of your life for examination. For example: your job.

Do you like your job?

Why or why not?

Do you feel validated?

Why or why not?

Do you feel valued?

Why or why not?

Do you value your work?

Why or why not?

Do you feel fulfilled?

Why or why not?

So on and so forth. Continue asking more questions that help illuminate your true feelings. The goal is to ask yourself both "yes and no" questions and "why" questions. Go slowly and deliberately; take your time with each question and really explore your feelings and thoughts. Do not ask questions that reinforce negativity, such as: "Why am I bad at doing _____?" This does nothing but serve to restrict your growth and development, and will prevent you from taking control of your life. Just like what was mentioned for the Inspiration technique, you want to emphasize productive developments.

You can do this with every part of yourself and your life, step by step, until you have a cohesive grasp on who and where you are at the moment. Keeping a notepad handy so you can document these inner explorations is a great way to be able work off of where you left off previously and track your progress. Don't shy away from hidden aspects that scare you; illuminate everything to your conscious mind. You will find that just the action of looking at what you're afraid of will help to make it smaller and less offensive. Once you discover what you value and like about yourself and your life and what you perceive to be negative presences in your life, you can work towards building the positive aspects and discarding the negative.

The initial attempt to perform mental housecleaning, as it were, will be the most difficult. If you are not used to this it may seem overwhelming. But as daunting as your mind and life may be to try to organize and analyze, you will find, as I did, that many aspects are interconnected. How you feel about your relationships affects how you feel about your job affects how you feel about your position in life affects how you feel about your relationships; what is present in one part of your life and mind will affect other parts as well. It's just a matter of taking those first few steps and pushing forward as the momentum begins to build.

Never think that you are "done" with any of these practices. As you continue to experience life, you will need to adjust yourself to assimilate what you have experienced. Continued mental analysis of yourself and direction will only help you progress further. It is similar to physical exercise except that what is developed is your identity, including your values, strengths, weaknesses, beliefs, and most importantly: your purpose.

CHAPTER 7

Establishing Purpose

ll of these techniques are forms of exploration. Exploration is a form of experience. It is through experiences and analysis of those experiences that we gain true knowledge. There are lessons everywhere, in every experience you may have, it just takes open-mindedness to discover them, and for most situations one or more of the three techniques–Confrontation, Inspiration, and Meditation–are adequate in helping to reveal the potential lessons inherent in the experience. It is only through experiences where we are tested mentally, emotionally, physically, and in our beliefs and understandings that we can truly begin to gain an accurate understanding of where we are and how we must improve in any and/or all aspects of ourselves.

I cannot stress how much negativity has no place in this process. You must remember that a person is nothing more than his or her conglomeration of actions. If you find you're not happy or proud of the person you perceive yourself to be or if you don't value yourself, it's only a matter of changing your lifestyle so that you're acting in a way that causes you to respect and value yourself. Remember that your position in life is important in order to gauge where you must go, but it is in the direction that you move that determines the quality of your character.

The goal for all three of these techniques is to provoke an analysis of what is good and true in your life. Through these exercises you can begin to develop and refine your understanding of self, the world around you, and what you value. Once you begin to determine what you value, you can begin to determine why you are here and what you must do with the time that you have. This is the beginnings of your purpose. Some of you may find that what you value is a humble existence, devoid of excess luxury, which is commendable. You may not want to strive to achieve a life of wealth. But let me remind you that being wealthy is not the same as being rich. You can move financial mountains in striving towards your goals while still living a humble, frugal life. Whatever the shape your purpose begins to take, you must develop it to a size that is beyond anything you could foresee being able to accomplish within your life. It must be the highest ideal of your life, a point always on the horizon to be working towards.

As you continue to "wake up," as it were, take control of your life, and shed limiting and negative thoughts, emotions, and habits, you will find that your perception of what is important will shift. That is how it should be. The point that you are ever working towards on the horizon will broaden some times and at others be narrower. This is a natural way to grow and progress, while always working towards what you feel is right. It may appear like a crooked, winding path in retrospect, but remember that you had to get to a certain point in one direction before being able to see that your direction needed adjusting. Learning is a process of picking up and dropping concepts of self and the world around you in a progressively linear way, as crooked as the path may be.

What is *not* okay or healthy is wild leaps in direction. You are embodying the Knight, not the mercenary. Do not be seduced by new and vivacious ideas. Your learning should be built on the addition of knowledge to your existing understanding or the destruction of concepts that have been proven false. Remember that the truth has no need to advertise, it is what it is, and anything that is sensational and overwhelming is usually attempting to hide its falsehood.

Once the quest, the purpose, is established in the heart and mind of the Knight, he'll fight with all of his strength tirelessly towards his purpose. This is a step-by-step process, for the path towards purpose is a lifelong endeavor. As one obstacle is overcome, another will be in the way. It is this continuous climb through little battles and accomplishing smaller goals towards one's highest perceived purpose that sets those that embody the Knight apart from those that don't, and subsequently set those

with power and control of their lives apart from the rest.
Tireless perseverance in the pursuit of purpose is what
makes a winner.

CHAPTER 8

The Shoulds

As you begin to put in the mental work to uncover what is true and false about your present position in life, what you believe your purpose is, and begin to establish goals, you will begin to illuminate exactly what aspects of your life only serve to prevent you from progressing. These limiting mental processes, actions, and relationships must be dealt with in order to grow and heal. One must develop the strength to do what he or she feels is right.

At some point you will have to confront the "should" voice present in your life, both from outside around you and from within yourself. The "should" voice is that which tells you that you "must," "can't," and "should," do something. It is the voice that operates outside of reason and desire, and proclaims that this is the way things will be.

We encounter the "should" voice very early in our lives. Schools and parents begin to teach us rules. Some of these rules make sense, such as treating others the way we would like to be treated, but many others do not, such as those attached to politeness and etiquette. A burp is just a burp, and it's only offensive in cultures that have decided that it's offensive. In fact, I have been to a number of places in the world where people pay no attention to burps, regardless of when or where they occur, and they don't seem to be any worse or better than people in societies that do.

As we grow up, the "shoulds" become more and more prominent: "You *should* get a regular job." "You *should* go to college." We begin to sacrifice more and more of our personalities, lifestyles, and desires for accommodating the ever-growing "should" voice that society provides and reinforces.

I'm not saying that you shouldn't get a steady job, or that you shouldn't go to college. What I'm saying is that you should (irony intended) be constantly and completely aware of the choices available to you and why you may or may not want to choose them. If going to college is right for you, then know that; make that decision completely yours. Not eating with your mouth open is a little shift in habit to adopt into one's life. Going to college or starting a career is a huge life choice. If you want a life of your own making, then you must be in conscious control of all of your decisions, especially the big ones. If one is not conscious of the ever-growing "shoulds" entering and controlling one's life as life goes along, at some point he or she will look around and realize that that his or her life is not anything like what he or she wants, and unfortunately the individual is not being rewarded the way that society promised he or she would be.

Because really, most "shoulds" come with the unspoken–or sometimes spoken–idea that even though you may not be happy doing this right now, and even though you may not understand why you must do it–whatever the "should" may be–it is still the right thing to do, and you will be happy in the future. I cannot stress enough how wrong that is. If you are not happy doing something now, whether it's a job or relationship or whatever it may be, then doing it over and over for the rest of your life will not make you happy. Happiness doesn't come from following the rules. Happiness comes from doing what's right in your heart, regardless of what the rules say. If you understand every aspect of what you're doing and want to do and why, then every aspect of your life is your own.

"But there are contracts," some may say. "There are laws and prisons." They're absolutely right, and those do wield some amount of power. I'm not condoning law breaking. I'm not advocating for complete chaos and rejection of society, partly because I don't think a life of taking from others and doing whatever one wants indiscriminate of how it may affect others is something that could validly be in someone's heart. But more so than that, regardless of what is in your heart, a disregard for rules still necessitates being as aware as possible of the consequences of your actions.

Every action has a reaction; it holds true in science and it holds true in life. While it is impossible to accurately predict the future, one must be as mindful as possible of the most probable future outcomes of one's actions. If you decide to rob a liquor store, understand that one of the probable potential outcomes of that action is that people might find you, potentially injure or kill you if you do not cooperate with them, and if you live and are found guilty of robbing the liquor store, they will put you in a big concrete building that you aren't allowed to leave for some time.

Contracts and laws cannot control you, they literally cannot make you do something or not do something. No rule, official or implied, can. Obligation is a false concept. The only power something or someone outside of yourself can have over you is to do something to your body, whether that's moving it against your will from or to a location, hurting it physically or emotionally, or depriving it of what it needs to survive. It is only in a small percentage of instances of being in the wrong place at the wrong time and in the most drastic of reactions that these power tactics are experienced. All that exists in your life are your actions and the reactions produced from those actions. If you want to have control of your life and happiness, you must develop your understanding of what the probable outcomes of your actions may be and follow the chain of reactions that pleases you most. The importance is that you act out of greatest desired result and not out of fear of consequence.

Society's Agenda

If you're reading this book, I can assume that you don't want to look at your life at some point near the end of it, whenever or wherever that may be, and realize that it has not been a life of your own making. Our lives are precious, both collectively and to ourselves, and it's a waste to concede control of them falsely and unhappily to aspects that have very little to no actual power over us. It is in the differences of those that recognize the falseness of obligations and the inherent power within each of us and those that hold onto living a life that they "should" be living that separates those that are in control of themselves and those that are controlled. If you want to be a millionaire, if you want a wealth of finances and quality of life, then you cannot be a blind rule follower.

This may seem radically anarchical to some, and indeed the idea has its roots in a survival, no-rules existence. But this way of thinking is also applicable to living very successfully within the social strata that exist. In fact, it is necessary.

Societies exist so that the individuals that comprise them can have some sort of support, understanding that there are certain overarching qualities and agreements that allow for one to turn his or her attention away from direct survival needs and towards other places. If you live in a society where you understand that (except in rare cases) people do not take stuff out of your house when you are not there, then you can spend your time away from home doing other things without the fear of losing your stuff. This is a huge benefit to the individual. The common agreements of society allow for a freedom one might not encounter if constantly fighting for resources. However, as societies develop and become more cohesive–especially with the aid of developing technology– society itself begins to require more and more from the individual.

In order for the society to continue existing as it is, it needs the individuals that comprise it continue maintaining its structure. Society needs people to work the menial, tedious, backbreaking jobs. Society needs people to work the middle class pencil-pushing office jobs. There is an incentive on society's part to keep people funneling into those jobs and lifestyles and keep them there so that the structure stays intact. If you do not take full control of your life, then you concede at least partial control of your life and livelihood to the whims of the society you exist in, and society does *not* want lower and middle class citizens to become wealthy. If you are to succeed in your life financially and otherwise, every action you make must be deliberate and of your own free will, regardless of society. Through acting with this understanding you will begin to see yourself as you truly are: Powerful, capable, and in complete control of your life.

Confronting the "shoulds" will scare some. Some people have lived their entire lives refusing to take accountability for themselves and their actions. They feel much more comfortable playing victim to circumstance and other's actions than having to be responsible for the state their lives are in. That's their decision, though there's little this book can do for them if they choose to continue existing in that false perspective.

This initial wrestle of control for one's life can be frightening. For many of us, including myself when I first actively began the journey to taking control of my life, having to wrestle control of one's choices and direction away from misconceived exterior stimuli and into one's own hands can be daunting. One loses the ability to use excuses, as he or she must assume complete responsibility for all actions and aspects of his or her life. While there is a beauty and satisfaction of knowing that every action made is accountable and justified in one's purpose and understanding of the world, there also comes a significant weight to every action as well. Many of these only affect ourselves, in which case we are the only ones that potentially benefit or suffer, but it is in dealing with others that careful and deliberate consideration must be made so that we can attempt to prevent negatively affecting another. That being said, it's impossible to never hurt another's feelings; there is no end to the different, unique perspectives of each person that prevents seamless and perfect communication between two people. Because of this, we must be willing to accept and deal with the consequences when we realize we have wronged another.

CHAPTER 9

The Apology

As you analyze yourself and life and develop your concepts of both, you may reveal times in your past where you have been at a point in your understanding–or lack thereof–that your actions have caused pain to another or others in your life. That is okay; learning is trial and error. Everyone makes mistakes. However, if you *do* come to a point where you realize that you were wrong at some point and subsequently hurt another, even though in that moment you might've felt completely justified, it is imperative that you take responsibility and make amends for those actions. It is only in openly amending your wrongs and false understandings in your past that you can process, discard, and seal them as something that is not a part of you in your present existence. This process of assuming complete accountability is a major step in becoming a Medieval Millionaire, and as difficult as it is, this is truly where the strength and perseverance of the Knight emerges.

One of the hardest things you may have to do in your relationships with others is to look someone in the eye, explain how you have wronged him or her, and then apologize. This is much more than just saying "sorry" and then walking away. This sort of apology is an acknowledgement of wrongdoing, expression of remorse, and then sealing that action as something you will not do again.

In doing this, though perhaps it feels as though you are laying yourself bare to another, you are in fact removing any power of your past to control your present. Similar to what is explained in the Confrontation technique, publicly acknowledging your wrongness from the past, explaining how you have changed, and determining that past action as something you will not do again cleanses your emotional debt for that action while separating your past self and present self. This also prevents anyone else from holding your past transgressions over you. If you have wholeheartedly apologized, then there is nothing more that you can do, and it is now the other person's choice to decide whether he or she will hold on to the past or move forward.

You may have instances when someone will not accept your apology, which is his or her decision to make, though you can do nothing more than respect the decision and walk away from the situation. To realize that you may have negatively affected someone to the point that he or she does not feel comfortable accepting your apology can be a shattering experience, but as long as you have offered a genuine apology and remorse for your actions, there is little more that you can do. Though perhaps not successful in fully amending past hurts, you have done what you could, and you can leave with your dignity intact because you did the right thing. While the few rejections of apology you may receive will end like this, you must remain wary of those who go further and demand some sort of payment, tangible or intangible, in exchange for forgiveness for an emotional wrong you may have caused. In becoming the Knight and taking full accountability for your life, you will learn to pay your debts as they are due, physically and emotionally, but only to the extent that you owe. The Knight is not manipulated into doing any more than he feels is right. Someone that demands either tangible or intangible payment in order to gain his or her forgiveness is attempting to exercise some amount of control over you. As the Knight, you concede control over you to no one but yourself. However, from personal experience, I will argue that you will rarely encounter rejection of a sincere apology and attempt at manipulation even less. Many will meet your apologies with appreciation and forgiveness. However, regardless of the reaction you get from apologizing, the action in and of itself removes the past's power over your future, and allows for you to more fully turn your attention to fighting towards your goals.

CHAPTER 10

The Backwards Path

n the age when a conflict of ideals meant a clashing of swords, being accountable wasn't much of a question. What use was it for one to potentially sacrifice his life for ideals and beliefs that he didn't truly believe in? Knights were willing to fight and die for what they believed in because they believed that striving for those ideals was the most important investment in their lives. There's not much value attributed to literal sword fighting in modern business and finance, but the same conviction of will and investment of energy is still necessary to succeed above others, especially in a day and age where there is little to no accountability and most are content with telling the occasional lie.

Beyond the inner struggles you may go through, you may also encounter outside confrontation. Others will notice your shift in demeanor and actions. If you are challenged or confronted, stand tall. Explain what you are doing and why. If you know these things in your heart and mind to be true and are willing to change them when they are not, then you have nothing to fear. Back to the concepts presented in the Confrontation technique, if you are willing to fight for what is true to you yet openly admit when you are wrong, then no one can hold any power over you. Trust me, this process becomes a lot less scary over time, especially as your perception of what your purpose is becomes clearer and you lose more and more of the extraneous clingers on in your life that are not useful or productive. At some point you will become fairly unchallengeable as you begin to embody a strength and responsibility that no one can find much fault in.

As the Knight, one must perceive life as an eternal battle. There is a whole world out there testing and trying the individual. It is up to the individual to take control of his or her life and confront the opposition. No one else will fight for you the way that is right for you. Similar to the desires of society, everyone around you is inherently selfish to a certain degree—we have to be in order to continue living. Because of that, everyone has an agenda for his or her own life involving him- or herself and those around him or her. Family members, bosses, friends— everyone wants something from you, and what they want may not serve your best interests. There is a constant push and pull between an individual and the environments within which he or she exists. If you are not willing to fight for yourself, your beliefs, and those other than yourself that you have chosen to protect and provide for, then you have no right to nor ability to become a

Medieval Millionaire.

Mental exercise on its own is not enough to succeed. The Knight is an equal combination of constant mental exploration and refinement *and* a physical onslaught to accomplish the goals developed by his understanding of the world. To be the Knight, one's mind must be constantly quick and moving, and one's actions must be deliberate and precise. This is true in combat, this is true in life.

The Backwards Path

The precision and power of your actions will come down to how well-defined and realistic your goals are. One creates well-defined goals in a process that runs in reverse to the "forward" motion of time. That is to say that one creates goals by first projecting forward and then working one's way back to where and when he or she is at the moment, instead of directly looking forward from wherever one may be. This can only be accurately performed by first having some sort of a concise established purpose.

The purpose is to where you will mentally project out to. No matter how grandiose or apparently improbable to attain, you must imagine a scenario where your purpose has been accomplished at some future point. From there you can establish goals working *backwards* from your ideal purpose being attained. Establish every step of the way, in reverse, from your completed purpose all the way back to wherever you may be in life at the moment. If where you are at the present moment is a point, and where your fulfilled purpose exists is a point, this exercise of establishing goals is drawing a line from the point of your completed purpose to the point of where you currently exist. To not inadvertently influence anyone's personal purpose, I provide the greatly simplified scenario of eating an apple.

You're at home and suddenly have the craving for   an apple, but not just any apple. The apple you want is growing on a specific tree 1000 miles away. More than that, there is nothing you want to do more than to eat this apple, and you want to accomplish this in the least amount of time possible. This signifies your purpose. You know that in order to eat this apple, you must pluck it from the tree. With that knowledge, you must establish the order of events from plucking the apple off the tree to where you are at home. The apple tree is in an orchard; you will have to get to this orchard. You figure that you will have to walk from the edge of the orchard to the tree (this will take about 2 minutes). To get to the orchard fastest, you know you will need some form of transportation other than your feet. You know the fastest way to get there is by airplane. With a quick check online, you find there is an airport 50 miles away from the orchard. To get from the airport to the orchard you will need a vehicle. You find online that you can rent a car from the airport for x amount of dollars that you can then drive to the orchard (this will take 45 minutes). To get to the airport, you must take a flight from your local airport, which costs y amount of dollars (and will take 3 hours total). Your local airport is 20 miles away from you. The fastest way to get to your local airport from your house is to drive, which will cost z amount of dollars in gas, since you are taking your own car (and will take 30 minutes). The fastest way to get to your car is to walk from where you are sitting to where it is in the driveway (which will take 30 seconds). So, working in reverse, you have worked out that it will take about 4 hours, 17 minutes, and 30 seconds total time and $x + y + z$ total dollars to get from where you are to the apple in the fastest way possible. If you don't have the amount of $x + y + z$ to spend, then you must further break down the process into the least amount of time it will take for you to accrue that money. Thus, you have reverse engineered every step of the way to get from where you are to the apple, and every step of the way is now a goal to work towards.

Understandably, the minor scale that this scenario is set upon drastically understates the amount of mental exercise it will take to work out the steps necessary to get from your purpose to where you are, and the scale of difficulty is even greater under-exaggerated in actual execution of these goals. Unlike the scenario, if you can feasibly foresee accomplishing your purpose in your lifetime then it is not big enough. Determining the best path from purpose to present is best accomplished through reflection and meditation, similar to that of the actual

Meditation technique.

There are an infinite number of paths one can embark down at any given moment, regardless of purpose, and even an amazing number of paths one could take to get to his or her purpose (if one had enough time), but it is by drawing the line backwards from the achieved purpose to where one is at the moment that illuminates what he or she can foresee to be as the fastest and most efficient route. To set out towards your purpose without this reverse navigation beforehand is akin to wandering aimlessly in the wilderness, hoping to luck upon your purpose at some point if you walk enough. To work backwards from where your completed purpose is to where you are now is to establish a path to follow, and gain some understanding of the obstacles you will encounter along the way.

Understandably, just like everything else about the Knight, this path is not concrete. As you progress down it, you will come across obstacles that you did not foresee and may be too big to overcome. If and when this happens, you must either treat this obstacle as a mini purpose, per se, in that you will have to break the path down from you overcoming it to where you are into smaller steps, or you will have to reevaluate the path from your purpose to you, finding a way to bypass the obstacle completely. Along with unforeseen conflicts and obstacles, your path will change as your purpose refines and shifts, causing the overall path to adjust in order to compensate.

Once this path is established, one need only to put in the hours and effort to walk it, climb it, fight through it—whatever one needs to do to stay on the path and keep moving forward. If you have put in the effort to establish your purpose and subsequently the path to take to work towards it, abandoning it would be the ultimate betrayal to yourself. However, if you have legitimately worked out what is valuable and important to you and developed a purpose based on that, then travelling along your path should be the most desirable and rewarding thing to do in your life. And with your purpose and path always available for edits, there's no reason why it should ever cease being the most important part of your life. If the path is there, it is just a matter of accomplishing the goals that will move you along it.

The Sword and the Shield

The Knight has two main tools at his disposal to use to achieve his goals: the sword and the shield. In our modern application of the Knight, the sword and shield translate out of physical items and into representative existences. The sword—what the Knight wields to slay that which stands in his way of accomplishing his quest—is his actions. Every word said, every action made, are physical manifestations of the Knight's will and only work towards his highest purpose through the goals that he sets. The shield—what the Knight puts up to protect himself from attacks that threaten to defeat him and everything he has fought for–is nothing more than his convictions. Through strength of mind, through complete and continuing development of understanding of self, the world, and what must be done, the Knight defends himself against all attempts at his destruction. If his way is true, then any idea thrown at him that is false will break against his inner strength and understanding. Any physical attempt to usurp his livelihood or assets is nothing more than a minor setback, if even successful, as the Knight will always find another way to accomplish his goals.

With a sword and shield comprised of such malleable and organic material, the Knight has full freedom and necessity to improve both weapon and protection. By learning through trial and error and absorbing as many lessons present in his environment as possible, the Knight can hone his edge so that he is continuously performing actions more precisely and effectively. By continuously testing one's convictions, the Knight's shield becomes ever-stronger in the face of opposition. It is in this constant improvement of execution of actions and strength of mind and will that accelerate his ascension towards his goals and ultimately his highest purpose.

The Knight's Code

However, beyond the strengths developed as the Knight, humans are still fallible and we are not impervious to temptation. This holds especially true when no one is watching. Being in control of yourself and your life also necessitates motivating yourself to do what you have decided needs to be done, even when no one is around. Some of you may have the strength of mind already necessary to set your mind to an idea and accomplish it regardless. Others, myself included, need a bit more to stay on track.

The workings of our minds, with their whims and emotions, are extremely amorphous. Rigidity and rules do not normally come naturally to the brain. Because of this, if one decides to have certain convictions and rules for him- or herself, it may be necessary to physically record them into a medium outside of the brain, so that they cannot fade, and cannot be bent as one may want to as they could be if they only existed in the mind. This is your Knight's Code: a way of tricking the mind into accomplishing whatever it is that you have deemed necessary.

As addressed previously, rules have no inherent power. Most people subconsciously attribute power to rules, accepting their authority and leaving them at that. Though I make a call to recognize the powerlessness of rules and to operate outside of what one "should" be doing, this power assignment of rules can be employed to help an individual. Because what you develop as good and necessary for yourself and your life is of your own making and not from an outside determiner, you can establish rules for yourself that you give power to enforce those desired qualities upon you from outside of the fuzziness of your mind. However, because these are coming from you personally, and because you already recognize the actual weakness of rules, you must keep a strength of mind that enforces the power of these rules. They will only work so much as you allow them to. If you decide to break your own rules then you are only cheating yourself.

The rules you develop will be truly your own. Perhaps you set a rule to not watch TV (which would probably be a very good rule). Perhaps it's never to speak negatively about someone when he or she is not there to defend him- or herself. Whatever your rules may be, they must come from what you believe is necessary to further your development and strength.

Just like with all aspects of the Knight, these rules cannot be concrete and unchanging. They too must undergo occasional analysis and revisions. However, this can't be done when one doesn't want to follow one of his or her rules, as the edits will obviously be influenced by ulterior motives, and instead in a time of objective reflection such as meditation. That way, one can objectively examine the validity and effectiveness of each rule unemotionally.

The Burden and Beauty of the Knight

The Knight is the most difficult of the three archetypes to put on oneself. It is a slow and continuous process of developing understanding and responsibility. But the Knight encompasses more than half of the work necessary to becoming a Medieval Millionaire. Strength of mind and convictions and the drive and perseverance to achieve one's goals are the main differentiators of the wealthy and the not. Once you know what direction you want to go and why, it is just a matter of executing your will in such a way that is efficient and productive. This is where the role of the King steps in, ensuring that one is using his or her time, energy, and material resources in what he or she can conceive is the best possible way.

KING

KING

One might think that the King is the most important of the three archetypes–Knight, King, Pauper–in becoming a Medieval Millionaire because of the regal association. However, while the three of them are all necessary, the King actually represents the least of personal transformation and growth. Without the added strengths of the Knight and Pauper, the King is little more than just an investor and accountant.

What does one first think of when he or she thinks of a king? Noble traits? Luxury? One doesn't usually think much of the business side of a king, but a kingdom has to be maintained somehow; his wealth has to come from somewhere. Our archetype of the King deals specifically with the relationship he has with his kingdom.

Historically, the king was the owner and ruler of a certain amount of land. He allowed people to live on and use his land in exchange for payment. These were his subjects. In return, a good king ensured that in times of trouble he could provide for his subjects, and when attacked he would defend his land and his subjects accordingly.

This is the basic interpretation of our King archetype. His subjects, while they can be people, are all of them investments, regardless of their form. It is into these "subjects" that the King invests his resources with the expectation that they will return more back to him than he put in. The King maintains and protects those investments (subjects) that serve him well, and they in turn grow and develop. It is through this development and management of valuable investments that the King is able to maintain and build his kingdom in size and value, to which extent is only limited by his ability to effectively manage it. In order to do this, the King must first understand the values of his resources, both for himself and others, so that he may use them most efficiently.

CHAPTER 11

Time, Energy, and Material

here are three elements that make up a life from beginning to end, simply put. The time that you live, the energy you expend during that time, and what physical materials you expend that energy upon. This may seem sterile at first glance, but this combination of time, energy, and material resources are also what comprise our thoughts, emotions and our relationships with others. The King is a careful manager of all three, as his time, energy, and material resources are what he uses to build his life and kingdom. Each have a different value to him personally and a different value to those in the environment the King is in (except for special cases which I'll address). Knowing what the values of each are, both to oneself and to the outside world will allow one to be able to get the most out of what he or she has with the least amount of waste.

The King's resources are divided up between inherent and accrued; meaning resources he contains within himself and those that he collects outside of himself. The inherent resources are time and energy. Everyone has a certain amount of time and energy available to him or her to use as he or she sees fit. The accrued resources are material resources that one may posses, i.e. money, food, property, etc. These are unequally divided and moved amongst individuals and their values are flexible.

Within these three forms of resources–time, energy, and material–there exist two hierarchies of value: personal and environmental. These two hierarchies illustrate what resources are ranked as more valuable to oneself and what are ranked as more valuable to the world around him or her. Thankfully, the personal and environmental resource value hierarchies are direct opposites of each other, so what is most valuable to the individual is usually the least valuable outside of him- or herself. This gives one the opportunity of investing the resources that are least valuable to him- or herself in order to return more less-valuable resources and/or retain those resources that are more valuable.

The Resource Value Hierarchies

We are only given so much time in a life. Though one can prolong one's life through healthy lifestyle, there's no definite way of determining when anyone might die. Because of this, time is our most precious resource, almost to the point that I hesitate to say that it can have a material value. Because of this, it is at the top of the personal resource value hierarchy. We should choose to spend our time where and how we desire, for to do otherwise is to waste it.

Conversely, our time is relatively worthless to others. Keep in mind that I'm only evaluating time, not energy, so this involves no movement or action at all. What good is it for a business or another individual to consume your time without gaining any resources of energy or material, except maybe to prevent you from doing something important? When you work at a job, you expend both time and energy, but a business will pay as little as possible for the job that you are working at. Your time and energy are not worth anything to the outside world compared to what they are worth to you, which is near priceless.

Energy is the second most valuable of resources to an individual. The energy that we expend not only takes up a certain amount of time but also requires our effort, which can range from minor involvement to exhaustion. Unlike time though, energy can be recharged with sleep and sustenance, and with careful planning much energy can be outsourced for what is required by some of the less personal investments such as businesses. Energy is the middle ground for both hierarchies, personal and environmental. However, your energy will be worth more to you doing what you desire than it is to another using your energy to accomplish his or her own goals. Those in your environment that see a use for your energy will attempt to use it for the least amount of material resources as possible in exchange.

Material resources are the least valuable of the three to an individual. You need a certain amount of food and water in order to survive, and shelter helps protect one from the environment. Material goods also help one enjoy life more, such as through vehicles for transportation, comfortable furniture, et cetera. However, for the individual, material resources only assist in further utilizing time and energy how one desires, whether through direct use–such as a car–or translated in order to free up more time for an individual or reduce the amount of energy expended in areas not desired–such as having enough money so that one doesn't need to work a job he or she doesn't like.

Conversely, material resources are the most coveted by most of the entities present in the world around you. Except for some rare cases, the majority of individuals value material goods very highly, more so than what is probably healthy. This harkens back to the "Of Money" chapter, where I call for a shift in perspective about money, the most prominent of material resources. Businesses also crave material resources. They want to pull in as many material resources as possible while paying an individual the least amount of money as they can for his or her time and energy for the sake of retaining said material resources.

What is interesting about these two hierarchies is that though the values are flipped, the inherent *power* of the separate resources are the exact same for both. Our time is most valuable to ourselves, but regardless of how we spend our time, we still must expend a bit of energy to interact with our environments. Thus, though personally valuable, time is fairly powerless. It is the energy that we expend over time that has more power. But energy is relatively powerless when exercised outside of the realm of material resources. Once one combines energy over time to material resources, whatever the form that energy or resource may be, maximum effective power can potentially be attained, regardless if it is applied in a business setting or in the enjoyment of life.

Businesses know this; this is why they pay individuals for their time *and* energy affected in some physical medium or on some physical materials in order to generate profit. That is why businesses have employees and the owners are not doing all of the work themselves. You must know this as well, so that you may utilize the inherent superior power of material resources–which we have established are relatively the least valuable to you– so that you may retain as much of your more valuable resources: your time and energy.

If time is the most valuable of the King's resources, and utilizing material goods has the highest potential for power, then naturally the ultimate investment for the King is one that requires the least amount of time and energy from him, and utilizes the relatively low personal value yet high power of material resources. This process of resource use and management is established and managed through the development of an efficient kingdom.

CHAPTER 12

The Primary Budgets

he Kingdom is comprised of the King, his subjects, and his and his subjects' resources. It is a combination of the King's self-control and effective management of resources and subjects that can cause a kingdom to grow, and possibly very quickly. Subjects work to provide more wealth of resources to the kingdom and are the most important aspect of accruing and maintaining wealth, but before a King can begin to construct his empire from the ground up, he must first evaluate his most basic needs and ensure that they are being provided for sufficiently. One has no hope for building and maintaining a kingdom if he or she can't maintain him- or herself first. This is done through establishing the King's Bottom Line Budget and Royal Court Budget.

The Bottom Line

In order to succeed, the King must first establish the Bottom Line Budget. This is the first of many, but by far the most important. The Bottom Line Budget, or BLB, is a minimum survival budget for the King so that he can survive and still effectively continue to serve as King. This budget serves the most basic needs of the individual so that one can always be assured that if he or she is making his or her Bottom Line Budget (BLB), he or she has food to eat, a place to sleep, and emotional/social validation and comfort.

One determines a BLB by asking these key questions:

• How much time, energy, and material resources are required for the King to eat?

• How much time, energy, and material resources are required for the King to secure shelter for himself?

• How much time, energy, and material resources are required for the King to be emotionally fulfilled?

I cannot stress how important food, sleep, and emotional fulfillment are. One's tools are only as good as one uses them. If you don't eat healthily, if you don't sleep regularly, and if you don't have love, companionship, and/or validation coming from some source–whether it's a friend, family member, or partner–your body and brain will suffer. *Your brain is your most important tool!* If you mistreat your brain and body, then all others areas of your life will follow in like. You will not be able to build and maintain the same scale of kingdom that a healthy you could.

Specifically figure out how much time, energy, and materials (chiefly money) are required for you to eat three meals a day, sleep well, and have some sort of positive social and/or intimate interaction with another or others. Break up the money needed for these things into the month. If your shelter takes the form of a mortgage or rent payment, factor that in. Break up the time taken for these three things into the month. You now know more or less how much money and time you need to secure every month to survive healthily.

For the reader that has no to very little material resources in his or her possession–really just enough to be scrounging from week to week–the BLB can be a careful evaluation of every penny spent in order to determine it's necessity. There will be almost no end to tightening the belt if need be. If you are low on resources and have few sources providing a limited income, then you can almost always refine your BLB to be more efficient. Speaking from personal experience, one needs surprisingly very little to survive and thrive. Once your kingdom begins to develop, your BLB may loosen up and breathe some.

For those of you who have some breathing room already or have developed your kingdom to a point to be a bit more comfortable, your BLB becomes less of a stringent financial diet and more of just a careful inventory of resources expended to secure these basic needs. How much you spend of your inherent and accrued resources on food, shelter, and emotional/social validation will be up to you, though you must be aware of the resources in your kingdom, these included, in order to always have an idea of the balance between what you are earning and what you are spending. For those of you that choose to spend heavily on these needs, remember that what you consume cannot be used in other ways. The more efficient and frugal the King is with all of his resources, the more resources he has available with which to build his kingdom. It is your self-control and restraint that will aid you in becoming ever-wealthier monetarily. That being said, humans are emotional and nurturing animals, and there may be those who you have decided to care for unconditionally that will also need a certain evaluation and allocation of necessary resources in order to maintain them.

The Royal Court

We addressed the falseness of obligation in the section of the Knight. After you have eradicated the false concept of being controlled by something outside of yourself, there may still exist certain things that you will still want to provide for, outside of obligation. These comprise the King's Royal Court, the "musts" of your life that you will not allow yourself not to invest yourself in. It might be that you choose to take care of an older relative or your children. In my case, when I was first starting out on my path, it was two dogs that I loved very much. Whatever the reason, once you have determined what it is that you want to serve, protect, and/or provide for outside of yourself, you must figure out a budget of time, resources, and energy in order to best accomplish these continuing investments.

The Royal Court is secured in the King's mind and life as more special and permanent than the rest of his kingdom. If you are truly dedicated to these special subjects, then your Royal Court Budget (RCB) will integrate with your BLB. In my month to month struggle of trying to make ends meet, there was never a day that my dogs weren't fed before I sat down to a meal, regardless of whether I had to eat instant ramen so I could afford their food. If you cannot dedicate yourself to something or someone in your Royal Court, then it has no business being in your Royal Court. If they're in, they're in. You must take ownership of what you choose to support. That is the Knight's strength and dedication in action.

If it isn't covered in your BLB or RCB, any additional consumption of resources directly takes away from you being able to develop profitable investments and subsequently your kingdom. That's not advocating that you schedule watching TV into your BLB, but that you stop wasting precious resources watching TV. This requires one to be completely mindful of how he or she spends his or her time, energy, and material resources at all times outside of the BLB and RCB. If this life is truly going to be your own, if you are intent on being in control, happy, and wealthy, you must become mindful of how and where you spend your resources, most importantly your time and energy.

You must always take care of yourself first before moving your time and energy to other areas. This is your life, your brain, and your body. Preserve and maintain them well and your life will be longer and more prosperous, emotionally and materially. A reasonable BLB is necessary for ensuring that you are doing just that. Once you take care of yourself, you will be able to take care of others. An accurate RCB will determine how much is necessary to do so. Once these basic needs have been addressed and budgeted for both himself and Royal Court, the King can now turn his attentions to what will provide the resources for not only his BLB and RCB, but also his luxuries and in fact all that is to be his kingdom: his subjects.

CHAPTER 13

The Subjects

nything the King chooses to invest in beyond his BLB and RCB is a subject. Who the King allows to "live on his land"–those subjects that he has invested in protecting and developing–are those that he perceives will provide a greater return of resources than his investment of resources, inherent and/or accrued. They can be people, properties, businesses–really anything. After removing the time, energy, and material resources the King uses for his BLB and RCB in a month, all the resources he has left can be applied directly to developing these investments. In order to affect the most from subjects, one must fully understand the nature of returns and how one can achieve the largest return to investment ratio, or the most return for the least amount of resources put in. This builds healthier and more profitable subjects and subsequently builds and strengthens a kingdom.

Returns from investments are almost never as simple as throwing money at something and then having more money. There is a great deal to understand about what one is investing in and what he or she can reasonably expect in return. There are Actual Returns and Projected Returns. There are single returns and recurring returns. There is a necessity for in-depth education about whatever it is one is pursuing, along with careful implementation of investment. As King, you must understand how everything in your Kingdom operates, both within themselves internally (if they are not people) and collectively as parts of your entire empire. Much of this comes from understanding the nature of investments and balancing them accordingly.

Actual Returns and Projected Returns

Subjects can have one or both of two types of returns: Actual Returns (AR) and Projected Returns (PR). These could be seen as the taxes a subject pays to the King, though the amount varies with and is dependent upon the individual investment itself. Actual Returns are those that actually return resources for your investment. If you have a job that gives you paycheck every two weeks, that's an investment of time and energy on your part that provides an AR. Investments with Projected Returns are those that you put your resources into expecting a larger payoff at some point in the future. If you buy a house and put some money into fixing it up with the intention of reselling it for much more than what you put into it, then that is an investment with a PR. Every AR initially starts as a PR, and PRs will eventually become ARs if and when they pay off, though only then, and should thus be treated as PRs up until then.

Relationships, jobs, properties, businesses–any investment might have some combination of both AR and PR. If you start dating someone and enjoy what you're getting out of the relationship immediately, that is an Actual Return for your input of time and energy. If you see the potential worth of further investing in the relationship for what might develop into an amazing bond, then that relationship also has PR. If you work for a mattress store for a paycheck but also think you have a good chance of climbing the corporate ladder, then that has some AR and some amount of PR. Homes and businesses can also have the same combination of Actual and Projected Returns. The point that I'm making is that most things you invest your time, energy, and money into can arguably have both Actual and Projected Returns. While ARs and PRs do not necessarily have to exist together in one investment, a kingdom needs *both* ARs and PRs in its total investments in order to grow.

Whether you start with close to no accrued resources and little to no kingdom, as I did, or if you already have some accrued resources and more of an established kingdom and you intend to grow your kingdom, you will always consistently need ARs and PRs. Actual Returns ensure that your BLB and RCB are at least being covered and then some, even if it's working for minimum wage in a fast food joint. Projected Returns are necessary for you not to be working in fast food for the rest of your life. If you focus totally on your AR–the paycheck that meets your budgets–and exhaust yourself every week meeting those budgets so that all you do is work, eat, and sleep–even if you are saving a bit of extra money every paycheck–then you will never have a chance to develop other subjects, those with PR. If you focus entirely on PRs, chasing a dream here or a promise of money there, with no regard for securing necessary ARs, then you are gambling your livelihood and what little or large of kingdom you may have away. Remember that along with the King, you are the Knight as well, not the mercenary, and you must be accountable and responsible for what you have chosen to provide and fight for.

Thus the goal, wherever you may be in life, is to establish a subject(s) who's AR(s) at least provides for your BLB and RCB while taking up the least amount of your most valuable resources: your time and then energy. Then your excess of time, energy, and materials can be invested into establishing subjects with significant PR. This means that even though you may be saving up some extra dollars above what your BLB and RCB requires by working 50 hours a week but don't have time to invest your resources otherwise, you are in fact hindering your ability to develop your kingdom. If you can, you want to take the cut in hours and thus the cut in money so that your BLB and RCB are still met, but that you have the *time* to establish more subjects with PR. "Time is money," they say, but it is up to you to determine how much your time is worth, not your boss.

Once you have an AR(s) providing for your BLB and RCB, you can then begin to approach how you're going to establish subjects with significant PR. Unlike ARs that either immediately provide a single return, or provide scheduled, recurring returns over a period of time like a paycheck, a PR can span a wide expanse of time before it is intended to pay out. The amount of potential amount of the return can also vary widely and the amount of work required to put into it can increase or decrease unforeseeably. This makes determining PRs a gamble, though ever less of a gamble the more that you know going into it. And if you have your BLB and RCB budget covered, then your livelihood isn't at stake and it's only a matter of making the best possible educated bets.

CHAPTER 14

Projected Returns

he wide range of possibilities in scope and effect of a Projected Return can make it nearly impossible to provide a succinct "how to" on affecting the greatest return for the effort. However, there are things one can learn to help determine what approach to PRs may be best.

Of course, the ideal investment is one which has the maximum return for the minimum effort. You definitely don't want to invest your resources towards a PR that is less than the effort put in. You must figure out the minimum you are willing to accept for your efforts. If you are working a minimum wage job for an AR, then you most likely don't want to accept less than a projected minimum wage payback pertaining to the time invested towards a PR after taking into account the value of the material resources used. Though it is impossible to be absolutely certain of the future, you want to use whatever information that is available to ensure that you are making the most informed decision.

Knowledge and wisdom are your best allies for working with Projected Returns. Knowledge about markets, costs, business plans, etc. is available from a variety of sources such as books, people, or the Internet. Almost everything you need to know can be found on the Internet or in a library for free. Doing the research beforehand will save you from spending your precious resources on mistakes after implementing the investment. But via the Knight, no matter how much you might prepare beforehand, you can still learn from every mistake that might happen, and the wisdom gained from real-life practice outweighs the information found in any book in value.

Determining in what area you establish your PR investment will be up to what goals, ideals, and purpose you determine as the Knight. There is money to be made everywhere. It is up to you to ensure that you are building your kingdom in areas which fulfill your desires and purpose. There's no reason not to do what you like.

The scope of the investment can be determined on a need-based approach. If you are lacking in resources and feel that stress of barely keeping your head above water financially, you will most likely want to start with smaller investments in both time and energy, and minimal material resources. If you have some breathing room then you can approach larger goals. All of this is left to your discretion and better judgment, and only trial and error can really teach you what works for you and what doesn't. I'm merely showing you how to build your kingdom, not what it should resemble.

Everyone has his or her own style to life. Everyone has his or her own approach. You will build your kingdom in your own unique way, with your own spin on the information I give you or that you find anywhere else. My goal in this section is to help you preserve what is important in your life and fully utilize the resources you do invest. In order to do that, you will want to design and implement subjects with the most substantial returns for the least amount of investment of resources. Subsequently, you will want "machines" in your life that work for you by continuously generating return, so that you can enjoy what you value most.

Jack the Carpenter

Just like an AR, a PR can also provide a one-time payout or a recurring payment. A single, large sum of a resource can be a boon to be used for immediately establishing other subjects. A recurring payment for an indefinite period of time can provide possibilities for long down the road. However, many times what might've been a one-time paying PR can be turned into a recurring PR, and indeed should be an option that is explored fully when planning for investments. I think the fictional story of Jack the Carpenter effectively illuminates the advantage and possibility of developing recurring returns into an investment.

Jack is a wonderful carpenter, able to build beautiful furniture. It's a hobby and passion of his in the hours when he doesn't work his nine to five. He usually builds a piece of furniture and then tries to sell it either to individuals, furniture stores, or online. His work is very good and his pieces usually sell quickly. Now he could maintain these fairly stable investments with a single PR for each piece of furniture–making a chair and then selling it–it does help bring in more money, but his Potential Return is only a one-time transaction for each piece of furniture.

Jack knows his furniture is high quality, and that it sells fairly easily. If he truly wanted to capitalize on his passion, he could instead spend some time, energy, and a bit of money building a company that makes and distributes his design and quality of craftsmanship of furniture. Dependent upon his past successes of selling pieces individually, he has a fairly good chance of creating a successful furniture business. Thus, he could no longer be building a single chair to sell, but spend his time designing and building chair prototypes and then having his business machine build many, many of those chairs. He can transition from many, single-paying investments to a single investment as a company that provides a steadily recurring return that is much greater than the combined single returns over time. Why build a chair when he could build a chair company?

True, Jack takes a risk with investing his time, energy, and money into developing a solid business plan, hiring on a few employees, and teaching them how to build the furniture to his exact specifications, but if his BLB and RCB are being met then what does he have to lose? He could make a lot of money and get his furniture into thousands of homes, and he still gets to do what he loves.

This translation from single return to recurring return can be found in almost every situation, it's just a matter of doing the work to design and create the machine necessary to make it a recurring return. Machines are what will build a kingdom most efficiently. If they are designed well and quickly begin to generate a profit, the hardest work is done at the beginning and the returns gained can be much more significant than single transaction investments. Your subjects should be working for you more than you are working for them, and that ratio should always be increasing, which brings me to the concept of Hardworking Subjects.

CHAPTER 15

Hardworking Subjects

nvestments come in all shapes and sizes, in all sorts of areas. Ideally, the optimum investment is one that requires the least amount of input for the largest return. This would be one that continues to generate a return without depleting the resources initially put in. These are self-sufficient investments, and the most valuable impersonal subjects to have in your kingdom. These Hardworking Subjects (HWS) are designed in such a way and implemented in particular markets that one only needs to do the initial work to establish them and then rarely have to touch them again, while the investments continue to generate returns.

This is how banks make so much money. They loan money to individuals and companies for the individuals and companies to expend *their* time and energy turning that money into more money. Those companies and individuals then pay the bank back the money that was lent along with interest. The bank has to initially invest very little into these transactions (excluding the money), and reaps a recurring return over time.

If a King were to create a number of these HWS, then he could continue to invest his time and energy elsewhere while material resources would continue to pour in as returns. The beauty of a well-designed HWS is that it requires very little attention once it is established. I've explained how time is your most important resource–you only get one life–and the primary goal of establishing a kingdom is so that you can pursue a life that you love and that fulfills you without wasting your time and energy in areas that you're not interested in. You logically want as many of the subjects in your kingdom to be HWS as possible, with minimal upkeep necessary, and in areas that you're passionate about so that the minimal time and energy used for upkeep is still enjoyable.

I'm not suggesting that you become a banker, though I'm also not suggesting that you don't become a banker. Being the Knight means that you already have personal desires, goals, and a path for your life. You have determined what you care about and what you are passionate about. With that knowledge you can facilitate the Knight's goals by investing your resources into areas that you feel happy and fulfilled spending your time and energy in. If being a banker is part of your path, then so be it, though there are many places to find HWS.

What can be used over and over without being depleted? Intellectual goods: music, computer programs, patents–any marketable organized idea that one can claim as his or her own. Books, even. Now I wrote this book because I want to provide anyone who's driven enough with the lessons necessary to become wealthy that I had to learn the hard way, but don't think for a second that I didn't think of *Medieval Millionaire* as a Hardworking Subject.

Intellectual goods have the ability to be replicated and distributed with usually only a single initial investment of time and energy, and with minimal amounts of material resources being used, and even less now with digital devices. If you create something of this type and it's successful, then it can continue to generate a return for you long after your initial investment of creating whatever it was. Intellectual goods are the simplest form of HWS and illustrate their power quite effectively. As they require some of the least amount of material resources to create, they can be an advantage for individuals that are limited in that area. But for those that aren't creatively inclined, there are still numerous ways that one can develop HWS of his or her own. Venture capitalism, renting of property, certain types of businesses; once the work is done to establish the form, structure, and operation of how the HWS will generate the return, many times it is just a matter of putting it into motion and stepping back.

There are plenty of informational resources available about every and any way you can establish HWS for yourself, though of course they won't be referred to as such. It is up to you to find them and figure out which ones are best for you and then work towards implementing them in your growing kingdom. This is where other prominent books on making money can come in handy, providing one with the specific knowledge necessary to navigate a particular market or industry.

Whatever the form your HWS may take, in order for it to be self sufficient, it must be designed and implemented in such a way that it is able to care for itself completely to nearly completely without your involvement. You must think of a HWS as a living animal, something that needs to be able to feed itself, protect itself, and do what it's intended to do without your constant oversight, all while being strong enough in what it does to allow you to reap some of the excess. The better your HWS is designed beforehand, the stronger it will be in its operation, and the less you will have to edit and amend the design as apparent flaws reveal themselves.

Though you will begin to generate more returns for yourself as you begin to add more and more profitable subjects into your kingdom, you will find that there are subjects that are not performing as well as they should, and others that are flat-out drawing on your resources without providing returns capable of compensating. There is an importance in doing some weeding so that your kingdom can thrive at its most efficient. This is the process of recognizing and casting out the Thieves in your kingdom.

CHAPTER 16

Of Thieves

nce you establish an effective balance of Actual Return and Projected Return investments with your time, energy, and material resources, you will be on your way to building your kingdom. As you keep working towards your goals and growing your kingdom, most of the subjects you integrate into it will become more and more impressive in scope and performance, as you will have more material resources to invest and greater knowledge of how best to do so. But of the investments in your kingdom, you will find that some do not provide as many resources back as you have to put in. These are the Thieves of your kingdom. The Thieves are leeches on your resources and detract from the overall health and success of the kingdom, and it is the role of the King to eradicate those that are not pulling their weight.

Thieves can manifest themselves in a number of ways. Perhaps an investment with a PR never paid off and you keep pouring resources into it. It is up to you to decide when you are done giving it a chance. Sometimes subjects with ARs become less productive and more needy, and the resources you invest begin to dwarf what is returned. However they appear, they must be dealt with swiftly. Similar to what was addressed in the section of the Knight, to hold onto something emotionally, regardless of it's value, will only inhibit your kingdom from growing healthily.

The "how" of dealing with thieves is difficult to convey. Each situation will be unique. It could be as minor as selling a property that is consuming more resources than it is returning, all the way up to a more drastic decision to sell or dissolve a company. Whatever the scenario, one must make sure to deal with the culprit in such a way that is efficient so as to not consume any more resources than necessary and so that it affects the rest of your kingdom the least amount possible.

Though Thieves may be addressed and dealt with adequately in your kingdom, you may still find that you're limited in time and energy to manage all of your subjects, though those remaining may still be profitable. This calls for potentially weeding out the least valuable of your subjects, both monetarily and in where you desire your attentions to be directed towards.

Survival of the Fittest

As your number and scope of subjects grow, you will come to a point where you have too many subjects with ARs than you have time and energy to maintain. It is up to you to determine which are least valuable to you in their actual returns, what you foresee for their future, and how much emotional validation you get from them. Those that are at the bottom of the list must be dealt with so that your time and energy can be freed up for more substantial subjects with ARs and PRs.

While it may be tempting to try and hold onto all of your moneymakers, you cannot let your greed control you. By not cutting the least valuable of your subjects in order to free up your time and energy, you restrict your ability to grow your kingdom, thus limiting future potential increases in wealth.

There is an alternative to cutting smaller, lesser productive subjects. If there are many of a similar nature, both in subject and operation, one can take the route of Jack and organize a few lesser subjects into a single conglomerate subject with a potentially higher AR to look forward to. I would argue that if feasible, this approach is more rational, though only if you emotionally value the presence of these smaller subjects in your kingdom. You get to keep the material returns coming from them (while most likely increasing the return to investment ratio as they are better organized) and you get to retain subjects with emotional value to you. That being said, there will still be some subjects you will most likely want to cut.

Remember the fast food job I mentioned earlier? If you get to a point where you are making thousands of dollars a month, week, or day from other subjects with ARs, but you still spend 20 hours a week flipping burgers for minimum wage, and you find you don't have time and energy to establish new investments, then I would expect that the fast food job would be the subject to hit the chopping block first, as it should.

The Royal Court Exemption

The Royal Court can and should also be put through a periodic evaluation as well, though one not focused on productivity. Your Royal Court operates with a separate set of rules than the rest of the kingdom. Anything or anyone in your Royal Court will be provided for regardless of whether they are drawing more resources than they are returning or not. Like what has already been stated, if they're in, they're in. However, it is up to the King to periodically reevaluate who and what is in his Royal Court and why. Children grow up, relationships change, and sometimes people that we've decided to provide for change to a point that they are no longer worthy of our time, energy, and material resources. Think back to the lessons in the Knight. You have no obligation to suffer negativity and toxicity. If you find that you no longer wish to support an individual, you must drop him or her from the Royal Court.

As you keep up with this continuing process of balancing resources between Actual Returns and Projected Returns while hunting out and eradicating thieves and cutting or organizing the weakest of the investments, you will find that–on average–the speed that material resources pour in at will increase. This is how *you* will determine how much your time is worth monetarily, not anyone else.

With this continuing growth in kingdom and resources, though the food quality may improve and the house may get larger, we have still left the King living off of his BLB. Undoubtedly–though I push the righteous agenda–one of the ultimate desires for becoming wealthy is enjoying one's wealth. Now that one understands the operations and structure of the kingdom and how to continue building it, we can now turn our gaze to what most people probably picked up this book for in the first place: luxuries.

CHAPTER 17

The Palace and the Famine

he underlying purpose of building your kingdom is to ultimately work towards your Knight's purpose, but in doing so also ensuring that you may enjoy life to the fullest. One can be happy living on a Bottom Line Budget, as I have been, but accruing an excess of material resources opens many doors that can free one to explore life and can help one experience it in richer quality (pun intended). As long as you are staying true to your ideals as established in the Knight, you should be able to enjoy the fruits of your labor, though within reason. This will mean different things to different people. Perhaps you want to travel. Perhaps you want a nice house on the water. Whatever your dream of comfort and luxury may be, it can be yours once your kingdom is sufficiently large enough, though it will take careful planning to ensure that what you do for yourself is fair to both yourself and your kingdom. This is achieved by establishing your Palace Budget (PB).

So far, just about every available resource of time, energy, and material that you might have has been called to be dedicated to effectively building and maintaining your kingdom. It is only once that mindset and process of development is established that one can begin to look at luxury. Many times–as depicted in the story of Poor Jim, Rich Jim–when people accrue money, especially when it's quickly, they begin to treat themselves, and quite lavishly. There is a necessity to being fair to yourself, but you must remain solid on your path as the Knight and just in your rule as the King. Like Jim, if you allow your greed to overshadow your purpose and your effort to build your kingdom, you will quickly destroy all that you have worked so hard towards, both in your moral fiber and your accruement of resources. That is why the Palace Budget must be approached objectively and carefully in order to maintain a balance of enjoying the result of your hard work while maintaining your uphill climb.

This is all said in fair warning, though I'm not going to tell you what to do with your money. What you do with your money is your own business. If you want to live large, then that is your choice. But be mindful of the fact that the more nonproductive areas that you tie your money up in, the less you have available to utilize for building your empire. I have already described the issues of consuming money over investing money.

I will offer you what I personally do with my money. The reason I include this is to illustrate a very powerful potential option you may choose for your own personal finances. You can review it and determine whether it's something you want to use for yourself. Regardless of your opinion on the design, it has been extremely effective in helping me retain and increase my wealth while assisting me in enjoying life to what I believe to be is the fullest.

Everyone will have his or her own approach to ruling his or her own kingdom. However, I believe that a strong trait of a good King is self-control while in possession of so much material resources. I personally take the approach that a King should only be as rich as his subjects. That way it is a direct incentive to continue building and strengthening one's kingdom. If your luxuries and pleasure are directly linked and equal to the average of all of your subject's excesses–their returns–you will work hard to bring your kingdom up with you in collective prosperity and health.

For those of you with minds geared for math, you may have already realized the interesting nature of limiting one's personal luxuries to the average earnings of your investments. In this design, the King can be fairly limited in what he is able to use indiscriminately of his subject's returns, and it becomes even more so percentage-wise the more subjects he possesses.

For instance, if you had only one subject in your kingdom and it had a recurring monthly return of $5000, then you would take $2500 for your Palace Budget (assuming you have a BLB and RCB of $0, for the example's sake), taking the average of you and the subject and its earnings.

That's 50%, as there are only two of you. However, if you had *two* subjects with a recurring monthly return of $2500 each, then you would take away $1666.70, a *third* of the total earned return ($5000), as there are three of you now. If you had three subjects, you would only take 25% of the returns. This can get even more restrictive as you have subjects with widely varying returns. Say you still have two subjects bringing in recurring monthly returns, but one is $2500 and the other is $5. You still only take away the third of earnings, which averaged between the two is $835. So the more smaller subjects you may have, the less your percentage becomes.

This may seem masochistic to some, yet the restrictive nature of this setup creates some interesting effects. One, it incentivizes a King to organize many smaller individual related subjects into single entities, such as what was addressed in "Of Thieves." This is purely for selfish accounting's sake, but in doing so this helps consolidate and organize a kingdom. Instead of having a slew of random investments existing freely in a kingdom, the King now has "houses" of investments, either organized under the structure of encompassing businesses or through other means, acting as a single conglomerate subject.

This also encourages the King to ensure that all subjects are earning similar returns. The average of $2500 and $5 is much less rewarding than that of $2500 and $2500. This helps ensure that the kingdom grows collectively, instead of lopsided and unorganized. This method also gives great cause to seek out and discard Thieves as soon as possible, as they are now truly a hindrance to the King by drawing on the resources accrued by other subjects.

This could be seen as a radical approach to personal finance (I would argue that this entire book is fairly radical), but remember, the money I don't collect for personal luxury doesn't disappear into the ether. All of that which doesn't go directly to covering my BLB, RCB, and Palace Budget goes to accounts that are directly applied to creating new and developing existing subjects. Considering I'm doing what I love every day, I hardly feel like I've lost that money, and keep in mind: if you're doing what you love, then many comforts, pleasures, and luxuries come in the form of business expenses used for developing existing subjects or starting new ones. A trip to Europe ceases to be a luxury trip when you meet with potential business partners. Get the picture? The Palace Budget directly provides for purchases, trips, and other luxuries that have no connection whatsoever to your subjects. If you are following the Knight in pursuing only what is important to you in business and personal life, then the two should blend fairly seamlessly and luxury spending completely separate from your subjects should be fairly scarce. True, it may be a stretch to justify a Ferrari as a needed asset for one or some of your subjects to perform better, but if you really want a Ferrari then you had better work hard and build your kingdom so that your Palace Budget can cover a Ferrari.

Keep in mind that even though one may be inclined to cheat in order to have luxury expenses be covered by the account reserved for developing the Kingdom, there is absolutely no illegal embezzlement happening. In reality, all of the returns that your subjects bring to you are 100% your money to begin with. If you decide to cheat, if you decide to try and follow the humble King finance plan and find that you are using resources from accounts other than the Palace Budget for unjustified luxuries, then the only one you are cheating is yourself. However, if you decide to step out of your kingdom and pull resources that are *not* from your own returns and instead perhaps embezzle directly from internal accounts from your businesses, then that is your prerogative, though you will be more than cheating yourself and instead breaking laws. But you are the Knight and rules do not exist, only action and consequence, though if you have truly developed the Knight in you I doubt you would allow yourself to such low falsehoods.

If you want this system of personal luxury finance, it's yours. This is something that I refined through trial and error. These are personal rules that I established from evaluating what I know and what I want to achieve. There is no obligation, here or otherwise; you are in control of what you earn. It is what I use, and I have become very successful in doing so. But regardless of the system you choose, if you are truly invested in becoming and maintaining being a millionaire, self-restraint and moderation are necessary. Otherwise, your kingdom can collapse under you, much like Jim. I encourage you to do research of successful kings, emperors, and leaders of any sort, historically, outside of the metaphorical archetype. Those that were most successful for the longest time, through good times and bad, were those that sufficiently took care of those under their rule and exercised self control in their indulgence of personal luxuries. Even though your subjects will be a wide range of things, more than just people, the same concepts apply seamlessly. And if and when hard times hit, if your subjects suffer while you are still living, well, like a king, then your kingdom will most likely fall out from under you. Which brings me to the concept of the Famine Reserve.

The Famine Reserve

A good King always has a reserve established for hard times. You want to be able to maintain your kingdom, even if only in a limited state, if you were to end up in a period of famine, where none or very few of your subjects were bringing in returns. This is the Famine Reserve. While this is an important budget to consider when developing one's kingdom, I decided to keep it out of "The Primary Budgets" chapter, as it deals with the kingdom as a whole.

The Famine Reserve should cover at least six months of your BLB and RCB. If you can and are willing, you'd be better off with a Famine Reserve that not only covered a full year of your BLB and RCB, but also took into account the draw of resources of your most prominent subjects with promising PRs, because if you were to lose all of your ARs in an unforeseen event, you would not want to be forced to abandon whatever PRs you had been working towards.

As much as one might be driven and dedicated to his or her goals, and as large of a kingdom one might establish for him- or herself, there is just no way to be certain of the future. The future is always full of surprises. Some are good and some others are small enough to deal with, but there will always be those that will shake your very foundation. While there is no way to be completely prepared for the unknown, you can make the effort to create some amount of security for yourself and the kingdom you have built.

The Famine Reserve doesn't have to be established all at once in one lump re-appropriation of resources. You can set aside an account or corner of the bed mattress to slowly start filling your Famine Reserve. Keep in mind that the larger your BLB and RCB are per month, the more you will need in order to cover them for the time span that you decide.

CHAPTER 18

People as Subjects

Much of the section of the King has used examples of subjects that provide returns of only material resources. However, almost all of what was discussed can be applied to relationships outside of those included in your Royal Court. Just like any other investment, you want to make sure that the resources you are putting into your relationships are returning something more valuable back to you. You want to make sure that you have no Thieves in your relationships.

As you begin to embody the Medieval Millionaire, you will most likely find that many will be attracted to you and your life, either by your new-found power and inner strength as developed through the Knight, by your wealth as judiciously developed and managed via the King, or by your skills developed as the Pauper, which we have yet to explore. Whatever the initial attractor, *many* people are seduced by money. It's unfortunate, but many relationships are negatively affected by the presence or lack of such an impersonal resource. Though relationships driven by someone's interest in your monetary wealth may bring you joy or some sort of validation, on behalf of the Knight and the King I stress that you should exercise extreme caution in embracing those who you can recognize are only there for what you have and not what you are.

The Knight in you would not stand for you sacrificing the genuine legitimacy of your life and actions for relationships so clearly based in falsehood. The King, though less righteous, would not stand to allow those with underlying greedy, selfish intentions into his kingdom. To do so would be to sacrifice the strength and security of the entire kingdom. You see and hear about it everyday–in the news, from conversations: rich people getting sued by family members, marriages ending almost as soon as they start with the partner getting half of the estate. If you're going to be wealthy and stay wealthy, you need to protect yourself. That being said, there's no reason why you can't have many beautiful and fulfilling relationships throughout the rest of your life.

There is something very important that I have learned from personal experiences. While most people may utilize the environmental resource value hierarchy–where they value your material resources above all else–it is those few who use the personal resource value hierarchy when dealing with you that will be the most precious. That is to say, there is no better relationship to have in your life than one where the person values your time first, energy second, and material resources last, if at all. True, every relationship has its weaknesses, whether it's a friendship, business relationship, or more intimate, but those that mirror your own resource values in what they can get from you are worth more than anyone that sees you otherwise.

It may seem impersonal and cold to regard your relationships as investments, but in essence that is exactly what any relationship is, save those of solid commitment such as what is present in one's Royal Court. The strongest relationships are built by reciprocating debt back and forth, regardless of the type of resource used. If someone loans you $1000 in a time of need, interest free, you now have a debt to him or her, but beyond just that of the $1000. He or she had no obligation to loan you that money, just as you would have no obligation in his or her position. You have accrued an emotional debt. Whatever the gesture, would you not be more inclined to return the favor when that person was in need? It could be as simple as someone lending you an ear to talk to or a shoulder to lean on when times are rough. Whatever the action may be, when you return these gestures and actions you pay your debt, establish trust, and open the door for increased emotional "lending," as it were.

It is through paying debts and providing emotional loans back and forth across a relationship that can develop some relationships into some of the most profitable investments of your life, though not in material value. But just like investments expected to provide an eventual

AR of a material resource, investments into relationships must start with someone taking a chance and putting in the resources to create an investment with a PR. Remember, all investments start with a PR until they pay. If you are strong of heart and house, then as a leader (for that is partly what the Medieval Millionaire is), you have the power to extend a hand to those around you and invest in others.

Life is about happiness–being content and emotionally fulfilled. What use are millions of dollars if you have no one in your life? Our relationships with others are the most important part of living. This is where the Pauper steps in, with the most important aspect of becoming a Medieval Millionaire: The worth of people and the power of paying it forward.

PAUPER

PAUPER

hat does one usually think of when he or she hears "pauper?" Someone that's extremely poor, perhaps. One that definitely doesn't have wealth. Pauper is a Latin word that literally translates to "poor." It was first used in a Latin phrase in the British legal system in the late 15th century to describe someone that didn't have enough money to pay for court fees. It ended up becoming a general term for the poor, destitute, and homeless. Indeed, I don't want you to be poor, destitute, or homeless. The role of the Pauper here serves as a perspective that will help you become unstoppable in your quest for a wealthy life.

There is a fundamental lesson to be learned from the archetype of the Pauper. The Pauper already contains the Knight, fighting for what matters most to him, and the King, so he has a handle on how to manage resources. These two archetypes already empower an individual sufficiently so that one might be able to begin building his or her wealth. However, the Pauper adds one last quality that not only ensures that an individual is the most successful possible in building his or her kingdom, but that his or her quality of life is also as wealthy as his or her material resources. That quality is empathy.

CHAPTER 19

Empathy

mpathy is defined by Merriam-Webster as: "the action of understanding, being aware of, being sensitive to, and vicariously experiencing the feelings, thoughts, and experience of another of either the past or present without having the feelings, thoughts, and experience fully communicated in an objectively explicit manner" ("Empathy"). Empathy is the ability of one to interact with other people emotionally on a level where he or she is able to associate with another's emotions and thoughts as if they were his or her own. Empathy is being able to recognize parts of oneself in others.

Why is empathy necessary? This entire book has focused on how we can develop ourselves, how we can develop our kingdoms, and how we can use the world around us to help achieve the goals necessary to do so. This has so far been a one-way street, where the individual is encouraged to absorb and use as much as possible of what is useful in the world around him or her. Not only that, but everything in this book has pushed for self control, perseverance, and using one's strength to achieve what he or she desires. One should be able to build a kingdom sufficiently without the help of others, right? As we progress down our life paths, it can certainly seem that way, especially if one has limited friends and family members present to support him or her. However, the key to understanding the necessity of empathy comes from the recognition that at one point we started with nothing–no material wealth, no knowledge, nothing.

The Power of Nothing

The Power of Nothing is a shift in perspective that not only allows one to fully appreciate what is present in one's life, but also prevents one from getting caught up on false pride, which is a definite way to stagnate one's growth of self and empire and cripple one's relationships with others.

The Pauper comes from nothing, regardless of where he may be. The Pauper starts on the street with just the clothes on his back, his brain, and his body to be used to accomplish his lofty goals and aspirations. Everything he might accrue for himself, whatever kingdom he may build, is more than he ever had to begin with.

We are *all*, in fact, born with nothing, regardless of how much money our parents had, regardless of the lifestyle in which we grew up. Be it orphan or trust fund child, we all enter this world with nothing. Up until the time we're old enough to get a job and provide for ourselves, someone was taking care of us, as minimally or comprehensively as that might've been. Not only that, while many lessons are organically learned by solitary trial and error, most of one's understanding of the world comes from lessons from another. While it takes a certain amount of drive and participation on our part, our development of life, understanding, and self are product of the gifts of others, be they caretakers, friends, or strangers. Wherever one may be in life, he or she is only product of his or her inherent drive of self-preservation and the influence and charity of the environments in which he or she exists. We have no ownership or entitlement to certain lifestyles, no matter how engrained they may be in us and though they may be all that we know.

Thus, the Pauper knows that everything he accrues–the kingdom that he builds for himself–is the product of two things: his hard work and the opportunities provided to him by the gifts of others. To build a substantial kingdom inspires some awe and pride at one's own inner power and ability, I know from experience, but recognition of the assistance of others offsets that pride. With the recognition of the Power of Nothing comes a deep and genuine gratitude and appreciation for not only all he or she has in his or her life, but for the people that helped him or her get there. These relationships and inner-dependence upon others not only holds for the individual, but also for the business, the country, and the world. The power in one's ability to build a life and empire lies in the power of the people behind him or her–those that have assisted him or her and those that he or she does business with.

The Power of People

Building a kingdom requires much from the self, though it is impossible if the world around you does not give you a chance. If no one will do business with you, if no one will meet with you or listen to what you have to say, then you can't do anything. A capitalist system requires at least two individuals in order to operate, though the one we exist in has a great deal more people than that. It is a system of moving resources, yes, but even more so, it is a system of people negotiating for what they want. At the most sterile, the negotiations manifest themselves as a price and the consumer's agreement to either purchase the product or not, dependent upon the price. However, that is only one small part. Business, both big and small, is built upon relationships between those with mutually valuable resources to provide the other. Buying and selling have their place, but the most notable business developments are based on conversations, actual verbal negotiations, and establishing trust and satisfaction among the multiple parties involved. This requires a certain amount of cooperation between individuals, companies, and countries.

Anyone has the potential to "win" in this system, though aside from the necessity of cooperation, to do so requires perseverance, self-control, and above all, knowledge. The qualities of the Knight, while developed internally, are product of provocation from one's surroundings. The qualities of the King are refined by trial and error in interaction with one's environment. The Knight and King are developed through analysis of experience. Knowledge is a direct product of experience.

This is your life, and no way of doing something will have value to you if it is not something you fully understand for yourself. That is to say, reasons and knowledge only have value when they are implemented through an experience in your own life. The first time a child may get into a body of water, he may be told not to try and breathe while submerged. Well why not? Every environment he has existed in so far hasn't hindered his breathing at all. The information is not enough; it takes the experience of choking to fully understand why.

This is true of all information. No information can nor truly should be implemented in one's life without proof of its validity. That being said, learning solely through experience is not only limiting but impractical. We know what plants we can eat because individuals in our species' past have figured that out already and others have shown us. We know how to build shelters because those more knowledgeable than us have refined the concepts of structural engineering and architecture. So there necessitates a use of learning through communication along with experience.

Lessons can be found everywhere and from anyone, either directly or indirectly. For the sake of retaining those precious resources, you do not want to waste your time and energy learning from your own trials and errors, if possible. With the knowledge that time is our most valuable resource to ourselves, one's emphasis in learning should be focused on using the least amount of time to absorb and apply the most amount of information. This limits the ability of relying on trial and error experiences significantly. Instead, one must look primarily to communicative, abstracted learning in order to be most efficient. One must learn through others' trials and errors. If there is someone from whom you are able to glean knowledge–either through subtle observation or guided lesson–then you can save yourself from using your own resources unnecessarily.

There currently are and have been quite a large number of humans on this planet. Do not think that you are isolated in your endeavors and goals. It is improbable that there has not been another person that has been down the same stretch of path that you're travelling down, whatever the direction. It is in your best interest to seek out those with the knowledge you want and learn to listen to those that offer advice, though as it has been stated before, it is up to you to determine the validity of what you're told.

Your business ventures–both in actual implementation and in your personal development of knowledge–are dependent upon and intertwined with others. You will not be able to do this alone, and the better you become at interacting with people, the faster and better you will be able to achieve your goals, not to mention the more beautiful and fulfilling the relationships you will develop along the way will be.

The Necessity of Empathy

Humans are social animals. We desire interaction with others, and we value it when it's enjoyable. Humans are also inherently selfish to a degree, though that's nothing to be upset about. Because of that, there is an inherent desire to both interact with one another congenially while also attempting to gain what we want. This makes dealing with others very accessible, as these common characteristics are at the root of each person. It just takes one human taking a leap of faith to give another a chance with the hopes of developing a relationship, one that is hopefully mutually beneficial. If no one were willing to take a chance on another, we would've gone extinct ages ago, with no development of language or technology to speak of. Thus, every person needs people to be willing to give him or her a chance if he or she wants to succeed in life. If every person needs this, then it also up to every person to give others that chance.

The Power of Empathy

The Power of Empathy is grounded in the recognition that we are all similar in our hopes and aspirations, though perhaps not in the way we strive to achieve them. Most of us truly want to be in control of our lives and to be powerful in doing such. We all want to be loved and to love, regardless of what some tell themselves or the world. At the root of ourselves we all want to be secure, happy, and healthy. You are not unique in wanting to be a millionaire, nor in your motives for wanting to do so, though not everyone wants to be a millionaire. Everyone searches for these foundational desires through different means, but the reality remains that everyone is working towards these goals, in one way or another.

The recognition of likeness in oneself and those around him or her gives rise to the most powerful and fulfilling tool in *Medieval Millionaire*: empathy. It is through empathy that we can find common ground with others. It is through empathy that we care for each other. It is through empathy that we can recognize the troubles any particular individual may be going through are something that we may have gone through already, could be going through currently, or will go through in the future.

To be empathetic to another–to recognize yourself in him or her, with the same fears and desires–and then to act with that empathy in engaging him or her blows doors of opportunity wide open in your life, the extent of which you will never be fully aware of. Unfortunately, it seems that it is a rare person that is actually aware of the necessary interconnectedness of people, and an even rarer individual to act positively to strengthen those connections. To act unbidden and unasked to help or genuinely engage another regardless of his or her foreseeable worth to you is like dropping little seeds, the future trees of which will be unknown to you until someone brings you the fruit.

The King establishes that anything can be seen as an investment, and one does better the more aspects of his or her life he or she recognizes as such. These positive acts towards others–these chances taken on other people–can easily be seen as investments as well. They have a fairly minimal risk and they provide returns, though the specifics of such are impossible to fully determine. These relatively minimal investments of resources provide an emotional AR: you feel good performing these acts, but they also provide an obscured PR.

A PR for an empathetic action may pay back directly–as someone you helped going out of his or her way to assist you in some way in the future, reciprocating emotional debt as addressed in the section of the King–or it may pay indirectly in some way unknown to you–as through your action of goodwill towards another person inspiring that individual to act the same towards another, and so on and so forth. Regardless of the way this PR may become an AR, you stand to gain some sort of benefit.

The potential direct PR is what gives you the most benefit in becoming the Pauper. Emotional debt, though never obligatory, is extremely powerful, especially when wielded in positivity. Individuals that have been helped or genuinely engaged with no expectation of exchange usually will want to go out of their way to reciprocate. Whether you disperse negativity or positivity to those around you, you will be met with like, and usually increased to a certain amount.

One must remember to never approach an action of empathy as a transaction. No one will want your "empathy" if he or she thinks that it's being purchased or that he or she is accruing some debt. You have no control over what others do so don't approach situations with only looking for what you can get out of them. Besides, to act positively and responsibly towards everyone you come across, regardless of what he or she may or may not perceivably directly return to you, is in your best interest.

There are 7.25 *billion* people in the world at the time that I'm writing this. 2.8 billion of those have access to Internet, per *Internetworldstats.com*. Whether you believe in the rigidity of the "six degrees of separation"–a theory that postulates that every human is separated from any other human on the planet via a maximum separation of six interpersonal connections–you must recognize that every day, through the advances of technology, our distance from any other person in the world is getting shorter and shorter.

This ever-strengthening connectedness makes positive interactions with others increasingly important. You never know when someone you have the opportunity to help could end up being a friend of a friend or a family member of a business partner. By giving your best to everyone you encounter all the time, you are ensuring that if that individual does turn up in your life through a connection at some future point, you have already made the best impression possible upon him or her. Conversely, to act negatively to another also seals your fate if you were to end up reconnecting with that person in the future.

This makes the presence of the Pauper ever-more necessary, and requires that those who embody the Pauper are constantly improving and refining, just as with the Knight and the King. It is a matter of trial and error and always looking for ways to improve. Each individual will develop this differently as everyone has his or her own personality and way of interacting with others. However, I will provide a basic approach that will help initiate interactions and strengthen one's connections with others.

CHAPTER 20

Becoming the Pauper

he how of implementing the Pauper's empathy will be up to you. We all have different strengths and different ways of interacting with others. Perhaps you might help someone change a tire, to go with the cliché, or perhaps it's as simple as asking a stranger how his or her day is going. There's no end to the scope in size or style of what you may do. This can provide a daunting amount of possibilities of how to engage another at any moment, so it is up to what one determines about oneself as the Knight that will direct in what way he or she chooses to do so. As there are so many possible ways of approaching implementing the Pauper, it may be best to first explore what one should *not* do, in order to determine what can then be done and how.

You will occasionally be treated rudely throughout your life. You will be rebuffed and rejected, for reasons you yourself will not be aware of. You may even be treated with hostility. All of these can come from complete strangers or from those who are closest to you. With those who you are closest to–relationships that are in your kingdom either as subjects or in the Royal Court– you have already been given the tools to determine what is necessary to do. But dealing with strangers is more complex, as the Pauper invokes a call to empathy and action, yet you have already learned that you have no need to suffer the negativity of others if you do not wish.

There are two options one can choose when presented with situations of seemingly unjustified negativity. You can react or you can act. To react is to meet whatever is presented to you with like. That is to say, if someone acts negatively towards you, you then react negatively. However, to *act* is to stop the chain of reaction and instead interpret the other's action through your own rules of engagement. Reaction is driven by irrational emotion. Action is driven by levelheaded self-control. I introduced the concept of the Knight's Code in the chapter: "The Backwards Path." I also spoke to the importance of un-emotional debate in the Confrontation technique. One can combine the two concepts into an explicitly defined code of unemotional, proactive interaction with others.

This set of self-defined, self-imposed, and constantly edited rules will prevent you from reacting, and instead cause you to act, powered by all the positive qualities of self that your progress has developed. If one of your rules is to approach everyone initially with kindness, then you will do just that. If one of your rules is to not suffer nega-tivity, then you will not do so. Those two rules alone will already allow you to approach everyone equally and un-biased, and then drop people and situations that return nothing but negativity. By developing a cohesive set of these rules in a specific hierarchical order, you can con-stantly keep them applied in your interactions and allow the actions of those with whom you interact to navigate the rules for themselves, without their knowledge. You will have to develop and edit these rules as you experi-ence interactions that do not fall into your existing set of rules and as you progress in life and understanding.

One standard rule for myself that has remained with me, unedited, for some time is one of the simplest. "Treat others as you would like to be treated." Perhaps it has been overused to a point that it has lost it potency, but it has existed for so long for a reason. There's a subtle power to it because as one's understanding of the world and self develops, how one wants to be treated changes as well. If you have taken on the challenge to become the Knight and subsequently become someone that you trust and respect, then that will be mirrored in the way that you interact with others by using this rule.

Whatever rules you establish for your interactions with others, they should embody a few key concepts. First, that you are approaching everyone with genuine positivity. Secondly, that in every interaction you are *acting* level-headedly and with self-control. And last, that you are approaching as many people as possible without significantly depleting your resources. It is in this last requirement that you will end up engaging some of the most unique people and continuously building your number of relationships: the most important aspect of your life.

Assumption and Restriction

This set of rules of engagement that you establish and act by can work wonders for your interactions with others. If you have established that you will approach anyone you see in need that you can feasibly see being able to help, then by your rule you *must* do just that, even if the person you approach appears to have the nastiest attitude from a distance. Of the negativity you will experience from others, not everyone who appears to be unfavorable will be negative, and some of the most approachable looking individuals can wield the most poison. You can cut out any chance of assumption by acting by a set of well-defined rules for your interactions with others, provided the rules are designed for that. You have the ability to force yourself to cut stereotypes out of your perspective just by forcing yourself to follow your own rules and having to engage people that you normally would not approach. By doing so, you create opportunities for learning, as we learn much more from new experiences and less from those that are habitual and comfortable.

By cutting assumptions out of your perspective and interactions with people, you are not only respecting the individual by giving him or her a fresh, unbiased approach, but in doing so you are probably interacting with that individual in a way that he or she may not be used to. Anyone with working eyes and mind can make assumptions about people. If someone appears to be nasty tempered, then whether he or she is or not, there's no doubt that others have picked up on that as well. If you are strong enough to act outside of assumption and stereotype, you become a very small percentage of quality of person in the world. Your initially positive interaction with an individual may be unique to him or her and could have a profoundly positive affect on his or her life, which as we've already explored has the potential to pay back directly or to live on in its own way after you've stepped back out of the picture.

It is by breaking misconceived or preconceived barriers and holding out a friendly hand, physically or metaphorically, that will take the world around you by storm, causing most people to not only respect you, but to strive to show their appreciation and help you in return when the opportunity presents itself. In doing so, you will have the opportunity to develop many relationships. Your proficiency of becoming the Pauper will determine the depth, size, and quality of your relationships, how fast they develop, and how numerous they become. The better the Pauper you are, the more fulfilled your life will be and the more successful your kingdom will be. Your life—both in the operations of your kingdom and in your personal well-being and happiness—is dependent upon these relationships, this network, and as I'll explain, this makes your network the *most* important element to your life.

CHAPTER 21

The Network

What is the Network?

Imagine yourself as a dot in the center of a very large piece of paper. Now imagine every other person on this planet as a dot on the same piece of paper. From your dot in the center, imagine a line drawn to every other dot–every other person–that you know. This is your network.

Your network consists of everyone you know–everyone you have ever met, regardless of the depth of the relationship. However, there is quite a degree of variance in the depth of relationship you have with these individuals. Because of that, each strand, each line connecting you and any person you might know, varies in width dependent upon how close you are with that person. Those you have only met once, never planning to see again, have the faintest strands connecting you to them. The individuals that you see or communicate with everyday have the strongest and thickest of strands.

The optimum network is the one with the most strands and the strands being the thickest possible. The more significant relationships you have, the more opportunities you have via these relationships to further develop your kingdom, both in business and personal life. However, it is highly improbable that one can develop a strong and meaningful relationship with all 7.25 billion people on the face of the Earth, so one must settle for the best network he or she can establish, and always be working to grow and strengthen it.

The network as a whole is best seen as a subject. With that understanding, one can use the same guidelines from the King in order to build, maintain, and strengthen the network. The King section addresses the issue of spreading oneself too thin across his or her investments, and the same concerns exist in building and maintaining the network. While most people that you only meet once and never plan to see again have a very faint strand attaching you to them, that strand eventually fades over time, though it never completely disappears. As any relationship between you and another is neglected or unaddressed, the strand connecting you to that person weakens and fades over time. These very faint strands do very little to nothing in consuming your resources over a period of time, so they pose no impediment, but of these weak strands, relationships can be developed as both people see fit, and it's those continuous relationships with interaction over time that *can* consume resources. One can easily establish a very large network consisting of very

thin strands, though it takes careful consideration of resources in order to grow the strength of those strands.

If empathetic actions are important, then utilizing the
power of relationships is even more so. Every person you
know was at one time a stranger, even those that you're
now closest with. Every big strand starts as a thin sliver
of a connection, so careful and persistent establishment
and maintenance of minor strands is essential in order to
have a network with many strong links.

If in your approach to a stranger you are able to build
somewhat of a connection, however minor that might be,
and you both find that you genuinely want to continue
interacting with one another, you have the opportunity to
initiate a relationship, as faint and weak as it may initially be. In doing so, you have created an opportunity for
emotional debt to be shared back and forth now, instead
of your positivity being dispersed blindly into the world.
But keep in mind that it takes two to develop a relationship, and to expect or attempt to force someone to form a
connection with you is foolish. That is why acting on
empathy is so important: you provide the opportunity for
another to *want* to initiate a relationship.

Instead of meeting someone once somewhere and then
walking away at the end of the interaction, never intend-
ing to interact with that person again, one could in fact
ask for or give some means of continued communication,
whether that would be a phone number, email address, or
some other mode of communication. We established that
Hardworking Subjects are the most desirable for achiev-

ing one's goals with using the least amount of resources. Hardworking Subjects can be employed in the network as well. Your HWS can manifest itself as a holiday greeting, birthday well wishes, or whatever one can think of in order to maintain contact with the minimal amount of work done. Though one might think that maintaining outlying relationships with the conscious concern of using the least amount of resources may seem cold, for most people, receiving well wishes and the occasional reconnection, as generic as they may be, means much more than eternal silence, as most casual interactions end up being discarded into memory after they're complete.

Once you develop some system(s) of HWS to maintain the connections you make with individuals, it's just a matter of keeping the information of those individuals organized in such a way that you can draw on them if you see a need. For example, let's say that you meet someone while on a trip in Atlanta, and you maintain a peripheral connection with him after you part ways. A year later you find yourself going back to Atlanta. It is now a prime opportunity to reconnect with that individual, even if just for lunch or coffee, just to check in and see how he's doing, while building the strand just a little more. You were going to eat lunch anyway; you might as well build your network while doing so.

Beyond casual interactions on business trips, your list can be used to more directly and efficiently build your kingdom. Let's say you need a graphic designer for a new subject you are establishing. Why not check your list?

You may already have someone in your network that you know, have a rapport with, and would do great at the position that you need filled.

Utilizing your list effectively is how one builds and strengthens a network. It's one thing to just have the contact information for a thousand people and an entirely other thing to have a thousand people looking forward to hearing from you and seeing you. The more thorough your information is on people, the more organized your list, the better you will be able to use it. If someone has dogs, write that down. You can mention them in the holiday card. The more you write down about a person–his or her job, birthday, family member's names, etc.–and the better ability you have to quickly find and access that information (such as the ability to search by city name, profession, etc.), the more information you have at your disposal, and thus the more opportunity you have not only to build your links with people, but also to find people that would be qualified to help you build your kingdom. And you will most likely shock and gain the adoration of someone if you mention his or her dogs by name in a holiday card.

It may sound like a lot of work to make connections and maintain them, but a good network provides more back than you put in. By keeping a multitude of relationships with unique individuals, all with their own strengths and predispositions, you can have at your call a slew of professionals and experts in many fields and an assortment of unique friends. Any new type of subject you may want to develop ceases to impose a steep learning curve if you have people in your network that can help you in designing and implementing your subject with their unique skills.

Networks also have an uncanny tendency to provide unforeseeable opportunities. Maybe someone comes to you with a promising business idea; maybe someone invites you over for thanksgiving dinner–whatever it may be, however big or small, people that you take time and energy to get to know and stay connected with will remember that and return that time and energy. And the beauty of a network is its unfathomable potential.

The Network's Network

Let's return to our dots on the piece of paper. You have yourself, everybody else in the world, and lines drawn from yourself to everyone that you know. Now imagine the lines of every other individual's network drawn on there. There would be so many lines that you wouldn't be able to see the paper.

It's easy to get caught up in what only we are doing in our individual lives while only regarding others as assets or liabilities to our own goals and desires, and the strengths of the Pauper tries hard to fight that. However, even with those strengths, it's a difficult exercise for anyone to try to visualize that every single person he or she sees in a day is just like everyone else, including the observer, in how that person has a life that is complex and unique, and that he or she has a full network of people with whom he or she has individual and unique relationships. It's an overwhelming understanding to remain conscious of, but regardless of whether one can fully fathom the depth of life to every person he or she interacts with, the existence of such has the unforeseeable potential to yield amazing opportunities.

Every person that enters your network, even if only peripherally, is not just a single person, but a black box of untold potential and opportunity. Every person is just as complex in his or her life as you are in yours. Returning back to the idea of the six degrees of separation, you just never know what your actions and relationships will return back to you. The people you invest your time and energy in have the ability to provide opportunities far beyond what you would expect or imagine. Take care of your people and they will more than take care of you in return.

You may be just starting out on your quest as the Knight, you may be only starting to build your kingdom as the King, but if you develop the Pauper's empathy and network of people, you will be propelled up through your goals faster than you can imagine, helped by the hands of those that care about you and want you to succeed. Of the three archetypes, the Pauper is the golden key to truly becoming a Medieval Millionaire.

MEDIEVAL
MILLIONAIRE

MEDIEVAL MILLIONAIRE

e have now covered the primary lessons necessary for transforming oneself into a Medieval Millionaire: someone that is powerful, wealthy, and living a lifestyle with relationships that are fulfilling and bring happiness. As you have probably determined, what the information in this book requires of the individual is significant. Learning and applying these lessons and shifts in lifestyle and perspectives is not something that will happen overnight. In fact, there is a lifetime ahead of you for you to ever-refine yourself in the ways that this book speaks of. As I've worked hard to prevent providing you with direct, specific advice attached to a particular way of life, much of your effort will be directed towards applying the information in this book to your own perspective and lifestyle. But whatever the path you take and however long it takes for you to accomplish goals associated with changes mentioned in this book, one thing remains concrete: in order to become the Medieval Millionaire, you must constantly be working to develop all *three* of the archetypes equally. It is not in your best interest to discard one or two of them to pursue a partial transformation.

CHAPTER 22

The Triangle of Success

ach archetype–Knight, King, and Pauper–
has its own strengths. When individually
applied to one's life, there is a potential for
significant growth as a person. However, all
three are equally necessary in order to grow in a complete manner and in a direction that is healthier than if only one or two of the archetypes were adopted. The Medieval Millionaire cannot be genuinely attained without constant and equal application of all three.

When applied equally, each archetype forms a point on a triangle, the Life Success Triangle (*Fig. 1*), in the center of which resides the Medieval Millionaire. Each archetype serves as a sort of regulator of the other two, preventing the strengths present in any one archetype of becoming vices. The absence of any one of these in an individual's ever-developing path will result in lopsided growth, the product of which will ultimately lead to a life that has some amount of restriction in the qualities of the archetype that was abandoned. To persistently work

Fig. 1, The Life Success Triangle

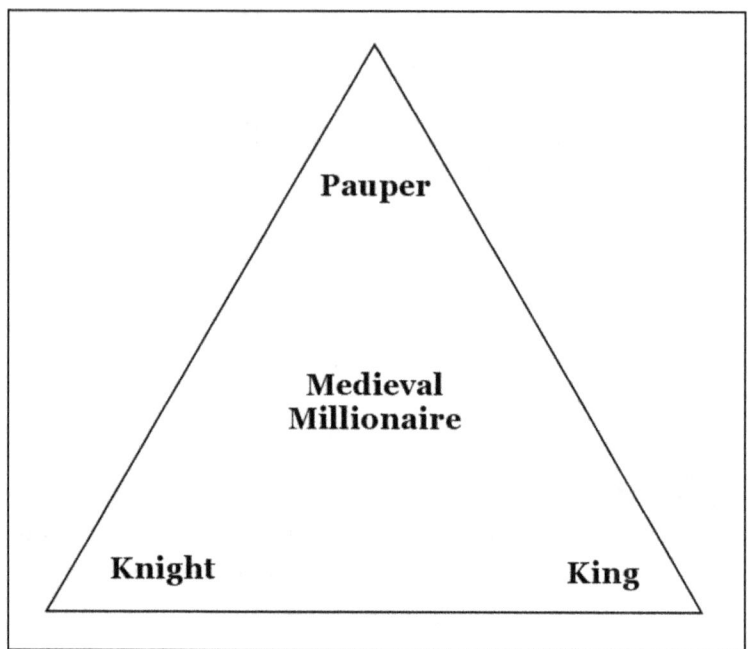

towards developing all three removes any potential restriction of how high you may go in your successes,
whereas only working towards one or two archetypes
will inevitably bring the individual to a point where there
can be no further growth in finances, self, or quality of
life. To illustrate the restriction of leaving an archetype
behind, I will explore the relationships between each archetype and the sort of character (or pair archetype) each
combination produces.

Each separate corner of the triangle brings a unique
skill set to the individual. Simply put, the Knight symbol-

Fig. 2, The Life Success Triangle with Archetype Venn Diagram

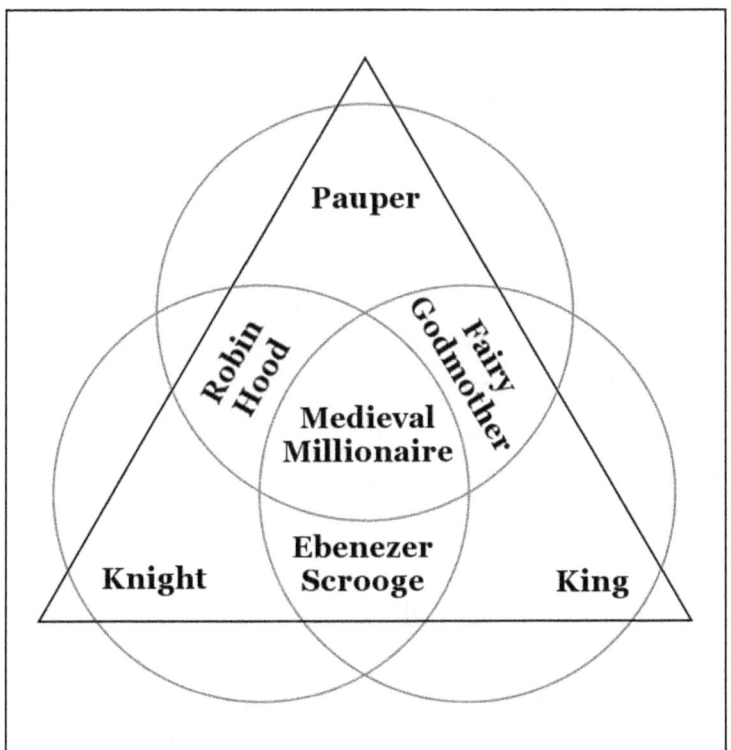

izes a continuous development of understanding of self and the world, defining and continuing to refine one's purpose, and developing the strength and perseverance necessary to work towards the goals that serve that purpose. The King allows one to prioritize aspects of one's life and resources, teaches one to find the most efficient ways of using one's resources to accrue more, and the importance of not suffering entities in one's life that only serve to consume resources. The Pauper illuminates the importance of relationships and kindness, helps one develop ways of interacting with others that serve to help and build relationships while transcending stereotypes, and teaches one the importance of efficiently developing the number and strength of one's relationships. The combination of working towards all three archetypes simultaneously yields the development of the Medieval Millionaire, but the combination of only two of these archetypes creates a "pair" archetype with it's own unique characteristics and limitations. They are the "Robin Hood," "Fairy Godmother," and "Ebenezer Scrooge" archetypes; represented over the Life Success Triangle as the overlapping sections of a three circle Venn diagram (*Fig. 2*).

Robin Hood

The Robin Hood archetype is a combination of the Knight and the Pauper. Robin Hood is widely known as the legendary Englishman that stole from the rich to provide for the poor, leading a group known as the Merry Men to do so. This combination of Knight and Pauper leads one to be very driven towards one's goals while maintaining strong relationships with others, with an underlying desire to do good for those people. But with lacking the King, there is no sense or desire for developing one's own kingdom or accruing and managing resources efficiently. Thus, while the Robin Hood archetype may be strong willed, personable, and charitable, with no kingdom of resources to utilize, there is a limit in the scope of good that he can do. And while not necessarily attached to the archetype, the real Robin Hood *did* steal to achieve his goals, which I would argue is an archetypically un-knightly thing to do.

The Fairy Godmother

The Fairy Godmother is a combination of the Pauper and the King. When one thinks of a fairy godmother, one is usually reminded of the old fairy tales, where a maiden in need is provided for by a benevolent maternal spirit with magical powers. From the perspective of the Fairy Godmother, she is one that provides for who she cares for as much as she can with the resources she has (traditionally being magic). As a combination of the Pauper and the King, our Fairy Godmother archetype is dedicated to helping those that she has relationships with, and has the resources and knowledge of managing resources to do so. However, with no Knight to speak of, the Fairy Godmother has no drive for her own life, and only exists to provide for others with what she has. Thus, she does not lead a life that is truly her own. And keep in mind, fairy godmothers almost always appeared in the fairy tales as static, minor characters. When have you ever read a fairy tale where the fairy godmother was the main character?

Ebenezer Scrooge

Ebenezer Scrooge is a combination of the King and the Knight. Scrooge is the memorable character from Charles Dickens' "A Christmas Carol," a cruel and heartless miser whose only intent is to accrue more wealth at the expense of any other person. The pair of combined archetypes of the King and the Knight is both adept at accruing and managing material wealth and strong-willed and determined to do so. But by lacking the Pauper, the Ebenezer Scrooge archetype has no interest in other people except from what he can get from them materially, and thus is materially wealthy but miserable and alone in life. I believe that most people that are interested in becoming wealthy and driven enough to do so also have the greatest risk of becoming the Ebenezer Scrooge archetype, thus making the importance of the Pauper even more dire.

Some of you may find that either at the onset of reading this book or as you begin to develop the Knight, King, and Pauper over time for yourself that you may sway towards one of the pair archetypes by natural preference, leaving either the Knight, King, or Pauper neglected. This is natural, as we each have different natural strengths, predispositions to habits, and ways of thinking. Some may be better at managing money than others whose strengths may lie in their ability to build strong relationships. Whatever the cause, in order to prevent becoming one of the three pair archetypes–Robin Hood, Fairy Godmother, or Ebenezer Scrooge–one must put extra effort into developing the archetype that he or she is weakest at. The Venn diagram provides an easy visual aid for determining what is lacking; it's just a matter of incorporating the original archetype that is opposite from the pair archetype you may be falling into.

Whatever your experience in trying to evenly incorporate all three archetypes into your life, remember that there is nothing bad or wrong with the natural fluctuation between archetypes you may go through. Though I doubt anybody wants to be Ebenezer Scrooge, being materially wealthy, strong-willed and friendless is still better than being poor, apathetic, and friendless. Any archetype you develop for yourself is progress, just keep reevaluating yourself to ensure that you are staying as close to the center of the Life Success Triangle as possible in order to become the Medieval Millionaire.

CHAPTER 23

The Four Books

By now you have undoubtedly begun to realize the amount of work needed to be done in one's life. There is mental and lifestyle housecleaning to do, getting to intimately know yourself and what you are here to do, and organizing your life, resources, and relationships efficiently, all while needing to reach out to meet new people and develop already existing relationships. That's no simple shopping list, and your path in becoming the Medieval Millionaire will necessitate careful organization and planning so that you may be able to develop the changes and integrate the habitual actions that are necessary into your life. On top of that, there is an added importance to tracking one's progress, not only as the King with his resources, but in developments of understanding and purpose as the Knight, and developments of relationships as the Pauper. This need for organization of everything about your life and simultaneous recording of progress and direction necessitates a system that allows for one to do this without consuming a great amount of resources. You may find your own way, but this has been done for me with the power of books.

I keep four "books" close at hand, and they track every and all developments in my life and myself in an organized and methodical manner. Three of them–of which I'll refer to here as the Knight's Code, the Kings' Accounts, and the Pauper's Network–pertain to each of the three archetypes and the developments and changes within each one. The fourth–which I personally refer to as my Pocket Book–captures all developments and pertinent information throughout the day to be added to one of the three archetype books accordingly. I also transfer any "to do's" or other necessary information from the three archetypal books to the Pocket Book. This system has ensured that I am not only organized in all aspects of my life, but that I am wasting no extra time in being organized, allowing me to enjoy life to the fullest.

If you choose to keep books of your own (which I very strongly suggest you do), you don't need to feel restricted to physical journals or ledgers. While I myself have remained fairly resistant to technology's development, many of these tools that I refer to as books can easily be established in virtual formats. In fact, my equivalent of the King's Accounts is primarily a series of Microsoft Excel workbooks. Whatever you choose, make sure you establish a system of your own that is comfortable for you in your life.

The Knight's Code

Of the three archetypes, the changes necessitated by the Knight are the most personal. It is an exploration of self and purpose along with processing what negative aspects exist in one's life and should be discarded, and what positive aspects exist and should be developed. Because of this, the Knight's Code works best in the form of a journal, capturing inner dialogue and stream of consciousness, allowing one to bounce ideas off the paper. This book is used to explore oneself and one's understanding of the world, what one feels is his or her purpose, along with improvements in oneself one can foresee that he or she desires and how to manifest them. This book also serves to establish and refine one's code of conduct in his or her interactions with not only others but him- or herself as well.

Using written word to examine emotionally and intellectually deep concepts can do more for oneself than unaided mental reflection and exploration. Forcing oneself to write ideas down in a coherent and organized fashion forces the mind to firmly define those ideas through the confines of language instead of leaving them as fuzzy thoughts to change and morph fluidly, as the mind does. It also allows for one to reflect upon the train of thought one took during a stream of consciousness and the path of development over a series of entries. This allows one to go back and compare and edit older thoughts and musings as they cease to be valid in one's present understanding of the world.

If you keep at it and use a physical medium to record your thoughts, you will eventually fill a book from cover to cover. When this happens (and you have a new book ready) this provides a wonderful opportunity to edit the old journal and transfer what still holds true to the new one. If you're persistent in your development as the Knight, much of what was written in the past will cease to be valid as you refine and develop your perspective and self. Thus, by determining what is still valid to you and only transferring that content to the new book, you end up with an organized and coherent understanding from which to continue exploring from in the new book. Upon transferring my current understanding and beliefs to the new book, it is my personal preference to destroy the old one, both to symbolically discard those old parts of myself for the current version and quite rationally cut down in content that might only serve to distract and clutter an already distractible mind.

The King's Accounts

The King's duty in one's life is to manage all resources and ensure that they are being utilized the most efficiently. This requires careful planning and recordkeeping. Thus, some sort of accounting must be kept of one's resources.

Of the time, energy, and material resources one accrues and spends, careful attention must be paid to make sure that one is staying within budgets and measuring return to investment ratios. This calls for recording all earnings and expenses. I personally write down all money that I spend and upon what it was spent. I also keep a careful record of what I earn, where it comes from, and I record the time spent working on different subjects as well. All of this information is recorded into and organized in Microsoft Excel workbooks, using formulas and careful arrangement so that I know what is being spent on each budget or subject and what is available. This allows me to keep a constantly clear view of what is the strongest (and weakest) of my subjects and subsequently where I'm losing money, if applicable.

Aside from careful recordkeeping of resources expended and accrued, you can add documents to the King's Accounts wherein you can work on ideas for new subjects. Into these documents go business designs, market research, projected overhead cost; really any and all information pertinent to whatever project you're interested in starting. This can help keep yourself and your potential future subjects organized so that you can effectively determine whether you have the resources necessary to invest in certain projects, and whether those projects have the potential to provide substantial AR. With having all of these projects organized and compiled electronically, you are given the opportunity to return to your initial notes to determine how accurate your plans and projections were for subjects that you have since established. This can give you an added advantage of helping you determine what you were right about and where you have room to improve and learn from your mistakes.

The Pauper's Network

As important as keeping your resources managed and accounted for may be, organizing your network is even more so. It is in your best interest to keep your network organized at the very least with a primary alphabetized list of everyone that you know and have contact information for. You can record as much pertinent information as you may have for the people in your network. This obviously includes names, addresses and phone numbers, but it also includes their professions, their birthdays, their spouses names (if applicable), their kid's and/or pet's names and species (if applicable as well), and any other important information, such as religious affiliation, hobbies or sports they may be interested in, any long-term projects that they may be working on–really anything that seems to be a prominent part of who they are and what they're doing. Most importantly, you want to record how, when, where, and through whom you met them. There is nothing stranger than having a condensed version of someone's life on file and not remembering how it is that you know him or her.

This information is gold, but only if one has a solid system of being able to access it. I would suggest that you keep a separate record that lists everyone in your network alphabetically by the city they're living in (though I only put the name down in this directory). I would do the same for professions as well. And on top of that, it is worth keeping a 365-day calendar where everyone whose birthdays you know is listed. I personally always check my calendar everyday into the week ahead so that I secure ample time if I decide to mail someone a letter instead of electronic well-wishes. These different directories will ensure that you have everyone's information organized and easily accessible depending on how you need to access it.

Though I would prefer to keep my entire network recorded in paper format, I also understand the fragility of confining all contact information for everyone I know to paper. Thus, while I still keep a paper record for my own comfort and nostalgia, I also maintain an electronic backup that I edit whenever a change is made to the physical directory.

The Pocket Book

Even though to reflect on one's life, progress, and goals is important; even though to keep careful track of one's resources and investments is important; and even though to have everyone in your network organized and accessible is important; I personally believe that there is nothing more important than the Pocket Book. As important as the three archetype books are, it is impractical to carry all three on you at all times, obtrusively pulling the appropriate one out to record information as it is needed. One needs a "hub," per se, that allows for information transfer in between your other books and your life that doesn't take up an obscene amount of space or time to do so. This way one can quickly reference or record pertinent information in a moment and then return to the more important aspects of living and enjoying life. Your version of the Pocket Book will be uniquely your own, though what it needs to accomplish is static.

This book is many things in one. It's part Knight's Code, as you jot reflections and musings throughout the day. It's part King's Accounts, as you record everything that you spend and earn in a day into this book. It's part Pauper's Network, as you also initially record new acquaintance's information into it. This book captures all information throughout the day that is pertinent to any of the other three books. Not only that, but into this book goes "to do" lists that are necessitated by any of the three books and immediate goals you may want to accomplish. This book is your everyday life and progress condensed into paraphrased words and numbers. Because of this, it should stay on you at all times. My personal Pocket Book is a slender 3"x 5" notebook that eternally sits in my front right pocket. Whatever form yours takes, it is imperative that this book stays on you at all times.

Personally, as I transfer information from my Pocket Book to the other appropriate book, I cross that information off. Also, as I accomplish items on my "to do" lists coming from any of the three books, I cross out those completed items. However you manage your own, if you are keeping up with your Pocket Book, then there should be little to no information that hasn't been crossed off when you get to the last page.

If you keep a physical Pocket Book, just as with the Knight's Code, it will quickly fill up. I maintain the same practice as I do for a full Knight's Code book. I reexamine all information in the old Pocket Book. Anything that hasn't been crossed out already that is still pertinent to my life (such as some longer-term goals) is transferred to the new book. Now my new Pocket Book has all of the uncompleted bits from my previous book, organized and refreshed in my memory, for me to continue working towards.

Getting used to using these books will take some time. If you're not used to recording your financial information or thoughts on life and purpose, then those habits will have to be developed. Just like any other change in *Medieval Millionaire*, it will take persistence and commitment. Before it becomes a natural and refined process for you, using these books may take some time. You will get faster as you get more comfortable with it and the process becomes a more concrete part of your daily life. Regardless of the initial frustration keeping up with these books may cause, the benefit of using these books is almost instantly recognized as one's life and mind begin to become more organized and efficient. This becomes ever more important as your kingdom grows in size and complexity.

CHAPTER 24

Sharing the Wealth

have now shown you all of the tools that I have to give you. You have read about how you can take control of and become accountable for your life and determine what is important to you and why. You have read how you can manage and use your time, energy, and material resources in such a way that works hardest towards accomplishing you goals. You have read how you can build relationships with others so that you have no lack of people in your life that will help you in your endeavors and provide emotional fulfillment.

What is in this book is precisely what I learned for myself and applied to my own life in order to become driven towards my goals, efficient, and loving towards others. This has resulted in my being financially independent and quite comfortable. I have no boss except myself, and I intend to keep it that way for the rest of my life. I have subjects in action at all times, and I always have plans for subjects for the future. I am surrounded by a very large group of people that are infected by my passion and my dedication for what I believe in and work towards, and I am constantly reminded by them how much they love me and want to see me to succeed further. I consider myself quite the Medieval Millionaire, with a wealth of material resources and an immeasurable wealth of the quality of my life.

You don't have to follow this book in its entirety. You don't have to follow this book at all. I meant what I said in "A Letter to the Reader," that I intended this book to be a gift for those who want it. It is up to you to do what you will with the information I have provided. You must make your own understanding of your reality and life, and if this book can contribute in any way, then I am honored to be part of that process.

I believe in what is written here; the proof of its effectiveness is apparent enough to me in my own life. I fully believe that if someone takes even just a part of the information presented in this book and applies it to his or her life, he or she will inevitably come to recognize the validity of other parts of the book. While the Knight, King, and Pauper were attempted to be presented as separate entities, they are all interconnected, and I believe that they are all present in the individual to a certain extent inherently. I believe that to consciously develop one will inevitably lead to some amount of development of another.

However, it is up to you to keep exploring within this book, in the world around you, and within yourself.

While I hold steadfast to the information in this book, my complete life experiences and perspective of the world is unique only to me. Perhaps what I have written is not the best choice for some. As the Knight, it is up to you to hold onto what is most true for you and discard what is false, this book included.

That established, I have one thing to ask of you, personally, from anonymous writer to unknown reader. To do so, I will have to disclose a bit more about myself. Part of my own self-defined purpose involves a dedication to help all humanity, in my own way, as I can. All of my subjects have that undertone, and all of them subsequently work towards humanitarian aims. I want to see everyone who truly desires it to be happy, in control of his or her life, and pursuing hopes and dreams unshackled by unfair limitations. This book is a direct product of that desire, and I offer it to the world in the hopes that it will do just that. Even if it just affects one other person positively so that in some way he or she is more capable, organized, or kind, then I feel like the time and effort I have put into this book was completely justified, earnings aside.

With that understanding, I unashamedly make the argument that if you do indeed find something within these pages that positively affects your life, then you have incurred an emotional debt to me. However, I do not want nor expect that debt to be repaid to me directly in any way. If you benefit from reading and applying the *Medieval Millionaire* to your own life, then please use what you have learned to help another. I came from nothing, and I figured out my path and the way to succeed through trial and error, analysis from those lessons, and the education given to me by the relationships I've had. This book was not there for me during my journey when I could've used it most, though I don't regret the path I've taken. That is why I have written it and why I ask you to share your knowledge with others.

What you do may be as simple as talking to a younger acquaintance that's just starting to try and make his or her own mark on the world. It could be putting your personal copy of the *Medieval Millionaire* in the hands of another that you think will benefit from it. Whatever you do, please make sure to spread the love and the knowledge that I have passed onto you. As you become more and more of the person you have dreamt of being and living the life you have always wanted, you have an amazing opportunity to share what you have learned with others so that they can do the same. Remember, we–people–are the most important aspect of anyone becoming a Medieval Millionaire. Thank you, in advance.

With that, I wish you a happy and fruitful life. May you be forever successful in your endeavors.

Glossary

Accrued Resources - resources that are collected throughout one's life: material resources.

Actual Return (AR) - a return that actually returns resources for your investment of resources.

The Backwards Path - establishing the path from one's imagined completed purpose to where one currently is in life in order to determine how best to work towards said purpose.

Bottom Line Budget (BLB) - a budget that covers the minimal amount of resources needed for an individual to secure food, shelter, and emotional fulfillment.

Confrontation Technique - a technique used to challenge one's understanding of self and the world via confrontation from one's environment.

Ebenezer Scrooge - a pair archetype that combines the properties of the archetypes of the King and the Knight, but does not contain the strengths of the Pauper.

Environmental Resource Value Hierarchy - a hierarchy of values for different types of an individual's resources as what is important to entities present in the individual's life.

Fairy Godmother - a pair archetype that combines the properties of the archetypes of the King and the Pauper, but does not contain the strengths of the Knight.

Famine Reserve - savings set aside significant enough to cover at least six months of the Bottom Line Budget and Royal Court Budget and the most prominent of the investments with Projected Returns in the chance of losing most or all of one's investments with Actual Returns.

Hardworking Subject (HWS) - investments that only require an initial investment of resources to become established, and then continue to generate recurring Actual Returns with little to no further attention or investment.

Inherent Resources - resources that any individual has available to him- or herself naturally: time and energy.

Inspiration Technique - a technique used to define what qualities one values in others and how to embody those qualities into one's own life.

King - an archetype one can employ in oneself to develop one's ability to manage one's resources in a way that is most productive and valuable to him or her.

Kingdom - all of the active investments of a King's resources that might be present at any moment.

The King's Accounts - a series of accounts that document all spending and earnings of resources within one's kingdom along with written documents for planning for new investments.

Knight - an archetype one can employ in oneself life to develop one's strength, drive, and purpose in life.

The Knight's Code (the book) - a book, either physical or electronic, that tracks the personal progress of developments of understanding, values, and purpose, along with containing rules of conduct for both self and those that one interacts with.

The Knight's Code (personal rules) - a set of self-designed and imposed rules that one uses to determine one's personal actions and one's interactions with others.

Life Success Triangle - a combination of the traits of the Knight, King, and Pauper, that when applied equally result in developing the Medieval Millionaire, which resides in the center of the triangle.

Medieval Millionaire - a combination of the archetypes of the Knight, King, and Pauper that leads to one being strong, judicious, and empathetic, thus resulting in one's ability to develop a life wealthy in both material resources and quality.

Meditation - the act of relaxing one's body and clearing the mind in order to organize one's thoughts.

Meditation Technique - a technique used to comprehensively explore oneself and position in life in order to determine what one values and enjoys and what one does not value and what negative aspects are present in oneself and life.

Pair Archetype - an archetype made up of the combination of two of the original archetypes–Knight, King, Pauper–that combines the properties of both combined archetypes.

Palace Budget (PB) - a budget of personal finances that delegates a certain amount of resources for the individual to direct towards luxury spending.

Pauper - an archetype one can employ in oneself to develop one's empathy towards others and ability to build productive, healthy relationships.

The Pauper's Network - An organized collection of all the pertinent information one has on all of the people in his or her network, accessible through searching by different parameters, such as location, profession, or name.

Personal Resource Value Hierarchy - a hierarchy of values for different types of an individual's resources as what is important for the individual personally.

The Pocket Book - a book, electronic or physical, that stays on the individual at all times and captures all

pertinent information in one's day that the other books–
Knight's Code, King's Accounts, Pauper's Network–
might require and implements goals into one's day by
what is necessitated by any of the others books.

Poor - those with little to no money and no wealthy
mindset.

The Power of Nothing - an understanding that one
comes from nothing, and is product of a combination of
hard work and the support of those around him or her,
thus keeping unjustified pride in check.

Projected Return (PR) - returns for an investment that
one expects to pay off at a future time.

Recurring Return - a return from an investment that
generates repeatedly.

Rich - those with money yet with no wealthy mindset,
thus only consuming money in attempt to get what they
want in life.

Robin Hood - a pair archetype that combines the
properties of the archetypes of the Knight and the Pauper,
but does not contain the strengths of the King.

Royal Court Budget (RCB) - a budget that covers the
resources necessary to provide for those that one has
chosen to protect and provide for.

Shield - the Knight's convictions as he develops his understanding of the world.

"Shoulds" - those things present in one's life or within oneself that dictate a command or obligation to do something.

Single Return - a return from an investment that only pays once.

Subject - something that one invests his or her resources into expecting a favorable return.

Sword - the Knight's actions as he works towards his purpose.

Thief - an investment of resources that consumes more resources than it returns.

Wealthy - those with a wealthy mindset that have the drive to work towards their established goals in order to develop a life of monetary wealth and wealth of quality of life.

References

"Empathy." *Merriam-Webster.com.* Merriam-Webster, n.d. Web. 23 Aug. 2014. <http://www.merriam-webster.com/dictionary/empathy>.

"World Internet Usage and Population Statistics." *Internetworldstats.com.* Data table. 11 Aug. 2014. <http://www.internetworldstats.com/stats.htm